My Golden Heart

Putting the Pieces Together Again

Sharron Magyar

Published by Motivational Press, Inc.
2360 Corporate Circle
Suite 400
Henderson, NV 89074
www.MotivationalPress.com

Copyright © by Sharron Magyar

All Rights Reserved

No part of this book may be reproduced or transmitted in any form by any means: graphic, electronic, or mechanical, including photocopying, recording, taping or by any information storage or retrieval system without permission, in writing, from the authors, except for the inclusion of brief quotations in a review, article, book, or academic paper. The authors and publisher of this book and the associated materials have used their best efforts in preparing this material. The authors and publisher make no representations or warranties with respect to accuracy, applicability, fitness or completeness of the contents of this material. They disclaim any warranties expressed or implied, merchantability, or fitness for any particular purpose. The authors and publisher shall in no event be held liable for any loss or other damages, including but not limited to special, incidental, consequential, or other damages. If you have any questions or concerns, the advice of a competent professional should be sought.

Manufactured in the United States of America.

ISBN: 978-1-62865-047-1

Dedication

This book is dedicated to all children who have been sexually abused -

especially to each child who keeps it a secret.

The author of this book does not dispense medical advice or prescribe the use of any technique as a form of treatment for physical, emotional, or medical problems without the advice of a physician, either directly or indirectly. The intent of the author is only to offer information of a common nature to help you in your quest for general well-being. In the event you use any of the information in this book for yourself, which is your constitutional right, the author and the publisher assume no responsibility for your actions.

Preface

Throughout history there have been many storytellers. Originally stories were told in person, passed from generation to generation. The beauty of those stories was that as each person told the story, the storyteller tapped into the energy and perspective of their generation. Stories grew and changed as another person added their own symbolism.

This book in many ways is the combination of different stories that are specifically designed to connect to your subconscious mind, much like the parables of the Bible purposefully speak to the subconscious mind.

As a consulting hypnotist I am trained to interpret symbolic language; I invite you to step into this metaphorical language so you may hear the story as it was intended. Each story carries a specific energy.

The other half of the book, the yin and the yang of it, is calculated to relate to your conscious mind. The conscious mind rationalizes the story directly so that you reason and analyze the book logically.

This book is composed of two parts. One part is story and the other is healing exercises to address issues stored in the subconscious. Although each person has their own reading style I would recommend reading the book in its entirety and then go *back and work the exercises. Embrace the ambiguity because the subconscious mind understands it.*

I give honor to all the storytellers who have come before me and to the reader. I value the energy that you bring to the reading of this book. Open your heart, mind and soul to the spirit and energy contained in this book.

From the bottom of my heart, I thank you.

~Sharron Magyar

Acknowledgements

So many people supported me with the book I can't name them all. Please know you are all dear to my heart.

I would like to acknowledge. . .

- My husband, Stephen Magyar
- My daughter Stephanie & her husband, Chad Hoover.
- My daughter Tammy.
- My grandchildren; Stephen Brown, Amber Hoskins, Morgan Hoskins, Cheyenne Hoover, Zachary Lyon.
- My sister Dr. Nancy DeLay.
- My x-son-in-law Raymond Brown.
- Alice Foster, Larry Creviston, Shannon Turnbull.
- My sound therapist, Teri Freesmeyer.
- My mother & father, Carmen & Oakley DeLay who always loved me and told me I could do anything.
- Mark Barlow.
- The Book Whores, my writers group.
- And, of course, Ann McIndoo, my Author's Coach, who helped me get this book out of my head, and my editor, Michaeleen McDonald.

Contents

Dedication 3
Preface 5
Acknowledgements 7

1 Soul Wounds 13
The Soul 14
We are born Precious 19
Energy 20
Birth Energy 22
Change 25
Change Is a Scary Place 26

2 My Story 28
Stress as a Dragon 35
One Smoke, No Pain 39
Choices 45
Time Stands Still 48
I Am In the Right Place 53
My First Hypnosis 55
Tammy's Transplant 56

3 Limitless Mind 61
Subconscious Mind 62
Superconscious Mind 64
Hypnosis 65
Metaphors 70
Time and Space 72
Milton H. Erickson 74
Trance and the Role of Ritual 75

4 Life Lessons From Houdini 79
Stress as an Addiction 83
Choose Your Words Wisely 86
The Power of Silence 88
Rhyming Time 90
Stress and Worry Are Best Buddies 91
Listening To Your Instincts 93

5 The Inner Child 97
Childhood Stress 100
My Inner Child 103
My College Fairy 104
Tammy's Inner Child 107
A Picture is Worth a Million Words 108
Inherited Soul Loss 110
Toxic Parents 111
Pages of Time 112
Tribal Connections 112
Trauma Imprints 115
Raymond's Inner Child 118
Frozen In Fear 119
Fear 122
David 123
Allie 126
I Always Believe I'm in Trouble 129
Victim Mentality 130
Lily 133

6 Broken Hearts 139
Conflict 140
Addicted to Love 144
Lonely Heart 148
Tomorrow 151
Gratitude 152
Detachment 155
Sherry 158
Zachary 160
Heart Songs 163

7 Family 164
Stephanie's Story... 165
Tammy's Story 166
House of Heartbreak 168
My Mother, My Mentor, My Friend........................... 171
Don't Ever Give Up 172
The Shadow of My Brain 175
Raymond's Story.. 175
Closure 181

8 Trauma..185
Shamanism... 190
Jason 192
Frozen Anger.. 194
Ghosts.. 195
Smacked Out Of Time... 198
Kinesiology... 200
Sound Therapy 202
Trust.. 204

9 Addiction..208
Coming Down 209
Lisa 210
Judgment 214
Hidden Memories 215
A Mother's Poem.. 218
My Child 220
Addiction: The Disease.. 221
Soul Fracturing... 222
Earthbound Entities 224
Angel Protection 225
Lies 226

10 Forgiveness 228
The Thief.. 230
God's Grace 233
Forgiveness for the Family 235

11 Ancestors 240
For the Children 241
Grandfather 243

12 Past Life Regression 252
Rob 255
Larry 257
Tammy and Raymond 261
Try Again 263
Angels 267
Tammy 269

13 The Golden Eagle 271
Today is Mother's Day 272
Grief 273
Tears 275
The Healing Power of Sound 278
Tammy 280
The Golden Eagle 281
30 Days to Live 283
Shamanic Breathwork 285
Mayo Clinic 288
Pterodactyl Era 290
Family 293
Gratitude Journal 294
I am grateful for: 294
Stillness 296
Final Note 297

1
Soul Wounds

Each individual soul originates as
a star in the night.

~Thomas Moore

Are you or do you know someone who is stuck in the pain of life? Many people have a broken heart they can't repair. Some are bogged down in depression that won't go away regardless of medication or counseling. Countless people feel lonely, or lost, or simply can't get over feeling hopeless. Have you ever been nagged by a persistent feeling that something unnamable is just "not right"?

Is your life out of control and you can't figure a way to change it, or do you know someone you want to help get unstuck in life? If so, this book is for you.

It is also for anyone who thought life was going to be beautiful, but instead was taken into the depths of despair.

I'm not going to tell you that all you have to do is change your thinking and your life will change (although that could be beneficial). This book is not for everyone, it is for those who want to come into divine alignment. This book may not resonate with your personal experience; however, it may be reflective of someone you know.

It is with humility and gentleness that I ask you to respect the experience of those to whom this applies. My goal in writing this book is to help you understand soul wounds, and to share ways you can connect to the subconscious mind in order to heal the soul. In doing so, you may more gracefully fulfill the far-reaching potential of your life.

The Soul

There have been many debates over the nature of the soul, but the common consensus is that the soul is the focus of the divine immortal spirit which survives after the death. The soul, the spiritual self, retains all memories and experiences of both your current life as well as previous lives. It is through the soul that we have inherent creative power which enables us to live a joyous life.

What gets in the way of living a creative joyous life is the ego. The ego often defines you and is disconnected from your soul. It keeps you locked into the idea that you are your past and future. It also believes that your body and personality is all there is of life. An ego driven life keeps you unhappy and fearful, disconnecting you from your soul's purpose.

Your soul gathers life experiences that can nourish or damage it, resulting in an accumulation or loss of personal will and power. You can generally recognize when you are gaining power by the positive attitude and success present in your life. However, we are unaware of our power loss because it often happens gradually.

All people have experienced a degree of soul loss.

For some, soul loss heals quickly and easily. For others, it has devastating effects from which it can be difficult to recover. Soul loss can diminish a person's ability to function on one or more levels - physically, emotionally, mentally and spiritually.

Physical, emotional, and/or spiritual wounds to the soul can be stored in the subconscious mind. Soul wounds have the power to derail your life and make you say and do things that drive you crazy. "Where did that behavior come from?" "Why can't I change it?" Soul wounds are a disconnection with personal power and with Spirit.

A soul wound can make you feel like you are stuck in fifty pounds of muck. The wounded person often knows something is wrong, either consciously or subconsciously. Until that wound is healed, carrying a soul wound can make you feel like you are emotionally or spiritually off balance, without knowing how to extract yourself out of the fifty pounds of muck.

How often have you felt you are out of step with everything and everyone? Frequently, people with soul wounds feel apathy, depression, anger, shame, fear and grief. These emotions can be crippling.

People with soul wounds sometimes say:

- I feel like _____ stole my soul.
- A part of me died when _____.
- I feel like I lost something and I never got it back.
- I feel like I'm not whole.

Other expressions may be:

- I feel like I'm in a dark hole.
- I haven't felt the same since _____ happened.
- I am numb.
- I am empty.
- I have a broken heart.

Soul wounds can affect your memory causing you to forget some part of your life, or a specific event. These wounds can make you feel spaced out, disconnected from life, and as if something is missing. Sometimes, merely remembering an event can make you feel stuck, obsessed, and unable to move forward. Soul wound memories often can catch you by surprise as they can be triggered by a specific sensory experience, such as a smell or a sound.

Emotions rule with soul wounds and often they are intense and disproportionate to the cause. They can cause you to feel shattered, overwhelmed, and broken by the intensity of the feelings. Emotions of hurt, fear, anger, and love often lean toward being manic. Many people with soul loss feel self-hatred, negativity, and depression.

A soul wound can divert energy from normal physical development, as well as take a toll on your body. Diverted energy is often used to encapsulate the wound in your body and store it in the subconscious mind. Energy diversion often manifests as apathy, listlessness, sleeplessness, low energy, and an inability to properly care for your physical well-being.

The greatest damage from a soul wound is that it diminishes your ability to:

- ♥ connect with your purpose on earth
- ♥ develop spiritual power
- ♥ grow as a human

There are a lot of self-help books that talk about intention, the law of attraction, and positive thinking with the premise that all you have to do is think it, and you will create a flourishing life.

As a pragmatist who has walked through the fire of life, I believe that all of us carry baggage that must be unloaded before we can draw the good life to ourselves. Creating through intention is almost impossible while packing soul wounds. Some people are aware of their baggage, while others are clueless. Self-help books are much more useful after a person has cleared individual soul wounds.

This book shows you how to survive the tough times, how to attract good things into your life, and how to step onto the path of healing your soul. The power to heal your current problems resides in understanding the issues that lie untapped in your subconscious mind. You can heal lifelong soul wounds by recalling and releasing your trauma.

Recalling and releasing your soul wounds can help you claim your natural birthright. You can spend your life trying to figure out answers to the questions – who and why you have been put on this earth? You are unique and possess the potential for fulfilling your destiny, but sometimes it is challenging to know how to transform into the shining light you are intended to be.

Each person's shining light can be dimmed when culture encourages us to deny our personal story. I say your life story is important and should be heard. That being said, it is the choices you make in response to your story that are significant.

We are spiritual beings with physical experiences born into the world with specific birthrights. We too easily give up on our dreams, and we are oblivious that the Universe is ready to help us fulfill them.

Or as Vincent Peal said in *The Power of Positive Thinking*, the secret source of energy in every great person he had known came from "attunement with the infinite." He believed that when a person knew he was serving a divine end, he was provided a continually renewing source of energy through synchronistic events that occur in life.

> Make your life easier and more effective by being in attunement with the "flow of the universe".
>
> *~ Loa Tzu, Tao Te Ching*

We are born Precious

Have you ever paid much attention to babies? They are precious. They demand that their needs be met, and are not bashful in asking for help. If they feel like laughing, they laugh. If they feel like crying, they cry. Babies are totally in the moment, and love filled.

As babies grow out of babyhood, they begin to be susceptible to fears and social dictates. The natural ability of babies to live in the moment diminishes as the ego moves into full development. As babies move away from the beauty of just being, they begin to lose their natural attunement with the Universe.

Working with the Universe, you join an infinitely greater power, and discover you are perfect, whole, and complete. Your internal wisdom knows that whatever you need arrives at the right moment and in the right order. The ancient philosopher, Epictetus, viewed that happiness comes from being in accord with divine intelligence, not struggling against the world or judging, but by increasing wisdom.

Victor Frankl tells us, "Everyone has his own specific vocation or mission in life; everyone must carry out a concrete assignment that demands fulfillment. Therein, he cannot be replaced, nor can his life be repeated. Thus, everyone's task is unique as his specific opportunity to implement it." You are a loving, joyous expression of life, and you are entitled to live life with positive choices and dreams. You can achieve genuine power by allowing your soul rather than your ego guide your life. Deserving miracles is your birthright.

Energy

We are energetic beings. Some of us may be born with higher energy levels than others, but the key in life is how we choose to use our energy.

Every thought and action carries energy. Holding traumatic events in your body and subconscious mind are huge energy eaters. Even though I am generally a high energy person, I was dumbfounded that after each personal trauma, I saw a reduction of my energy. Just doing the normal things that I always took for granted became a chore. My own personal experience has been informative and enlightening. I can now empathize with people who complain they just don't have the energy to do what they want.

Many times we set ourselves up for energy loss through our thoughts and actions. We often behave in negative ways, because we have particular thoughts that over our lifetime grow to become habitual. Persistent negative patterns of thought will begin to lose their power over your life once you become aware they exist.

The following lists ways energy can be squandered:

- 💗 Dwelling on past events or past experiences.
- 💗 Complaining.
- 💗 Focusing on negative thoughts.
- 💗 Using energy to hold up defense mechanisms.
- 💗 Using energy to defend the ego.
- 💗 Making poor self-choices (ex: smoking, substance abuse, non-supportive eating choices, lack of exercise.)

In every interaction between people, there is an exchange of energy. Is there a serious imbalance in the energy exchange in your relationships? Do you take others' energy by complaining? If you do, people will eventually move out of a relationship with you.

Conversely, do you allow others to take all your energy leaving you depleted? If you do, you may eventually choose to get out of the relationship. The following soul exercise can help you put your relationships into energetic perspective.

Soul Exercise # 1: Energy Exchange

Always do meditation in a relaxing, private place. You may tape record this meditation and play it back.

Take a deep breath. Inhale deeply into your belly for seven counts; hold your breath for seven counts; exhale for seven counts, and hold for seven counts. Repeat this process seven times. Focus on releasing all negativity while exhaling. Breathe in tranquility and peace as you inhale. Breathe out stress and tension as you exhale. Eventually, you will step into a natural breathing rhythm and fall into a deep relaxation.

When fully relaxed practice imagining energy exchanges in your relationships to find the imbalances. Are you giving too much energy, are you taking too much energy, or is there an equal exchange of energy? If you are the one who constantly gives energy, the result can be burnout and an overwhelmed feeling. If you allow others to always take your energy, it can take a toll on your self-esteem and cause reduced or depleted energy. If you are a taker of energy, you've set yourself up for loneliness.

In your mind, imagine an equal exchange of energy between you and each of your relationships. Becoming aware of your energy is pivotal to personal transformation.

Practice this exercise every night before sleeping until you step into a more appropriate energy exchange in your relationships. When you feel the process is completed, breathe deeply, and count to five, then bring your awareness back to the room. (Warning: Sometimes you may have to choose to let go of a relationship if they continually take your energy.)

Birth Energy

Birth energy is the energy carried to your conception by your father and mother. This energy can impact you in childhood and throughout your life by influencing the development of your life force energy and your personality.

If I asked if you knew a child born with high energy, most people could answer "yes." A child that has been loved throughout childhood generally maintains a high energy level. Energy accumulated from being nurtured encourages a child to develop into a productive adult. In comparing a nurtured child to one who has been abused, we see incredibly different energy levels.

An abused child's energy is often diverted to contain the abusive experience in the subconscious mind. One of the functions of the subconscious mind is to store information where it can be retrieved by the conscious mind when it needs to defend itself for survival (an example is the activation of the fight or flight response).

The subconscious will also store information it cannot immediately process or fully understand. When energy is diverted in childhood, it often produces low energy which can result in a tendency toward depression in adulthood. Energy diversion blocks learning and is often at the foundation of an abused child's inability to organize and prioritize.

What matters with birth energy is how you choose to use your energy. You can be born with high energy and squander it through negative life choices and experiences. On the opposite side, you may be born with low energy and increase your energy through positive choices and life experiences. A child who is loved and carefully nourished throughout childhood without experiencing trauma accumulates energy.

As an analogy, if an appliance was improperly wired, it would sporadically use energy or explode from too much energy. Our explosions as humans manifest as nervous breakdowns, panic attacks, bipolar episodes, and other mental illnesses; all are directly related to either not enough energy, or too much energy flowing into the body.

Another important consideration in varying levels of birth energy is that the energy can be related to past life experiences. You can become stuck in a denser energetic level in your current life, if in a past life you were involved in black magic or committed atrocities against mankind. Part of your current life challenge would be to bring energetic balance into both lifetimes.

On the other hand, if you made accomplishments to assist mankind in some manner in a past life, you can be born on a lighter energetic level in your current life.

An extraordinary event in your current life can propel you to a higher, lighter energetic level. If you are living in a higher energetic level you will feel positive and connect to the Universe to provide for your needs. A traumatic experience can push a person into a denser, darker energetic level. An example is: A child born on a higher energetic plane who has experienced sexual abuse can be pushed to a lower, denser energetic level. Additionally, addiction and illness can lower your energetic level. You can experience depression and an inability to manifest good things in your life, in a denser energetic level.

It is also possible to intentionally raise or lower your energetic level through positive choices and actions. Monks are a prime example of people who raise their energetic level through meditation and chanting. Anything requiring the use of the creative mind, such as dance, music, exercises, and art, can raise an individual's energetic level.

You generally seek people in the same energetic level as you in your life relationships. If you are on a lighter energetic level, it is difficult for you to understand another person's experiences that occur on a denser energetic level, and vice versa.

Most people don't recognize the affects of energy in their life. It is complicated: you can feel it, but you can't see it. Ask anyone if they have high or low energy, and they can give you an answer. Energetic modalities such as self-hypnosis, massage, and meditation, as well as exercise regimes including tai chi, chi qigong, and yoga help regulate and balance the flow of energy in your body more evenly.

Change

~Sharron Magyar

Change; a scary place,

Shadows of a past I cannot embrace,

Anxiety I cannot change, worry all over my face.

The future, a dark hole in my soul

Calling me from whom I really am;

Walls up to protect this place, life without grace.

Change; can I be content living in this internment?

I ask the Universe to give me grace

To make the changes to leave this scary place.

Change Is a Scary Place

What keeps us stuck in soul wounds? Often, it is our resistance to change. Virginia Satir noted that the strongest instinct in human beings is the instinct to keep things familiar. Because familiarity makes us feel secure, we may continually repeat behavior even if it has negative consequences.

Change can often be scary. The challenge to change your existing belief system (even when old concepts no longer work for you) can be frightening. You initiate change when you're willing to say, "I don't want to live like this anymore."

We can make the decision to change, or life can make that choice for us, by handing us catastrophic events that force us out of our comfort zone. People who do not acknowledge, embrace, and integrate spontaneous changes are sentenced to living an uncreative way of life in an outmoded past. (Rossi, 1972/1975)

People frequently stick to their habits until they're forced to change . . . or they die to keep from changing. My husband smoked; he knew he needed to quit. It wasn't until he had open heart surgery, and the doctor said, "You have smoked your last cigarette," that he actually made the change. Addictions can be so strong that many smokers make the choice to die rather than change into a non-smoker.

When you are in tune with the Universe, the right teachers enter your life to support the change you choose. On a personal note - I was walking across a street one day when

I was run over by a car which trashed my body. A series of alternative healers came into my life to assist with my recovery. I did not seek them out, they presented themselves, one by one, and in the healing sequence I needed them. In making change, I was given lessons and opportunities for personal growth while I discovered the many faceted human that I am.

I believe we each are born with power and intelligence. Sometimes, however, life delivers difficult experiences to provide for the growth of the soul. Included in this book are other people's courageous stories of their connection to love and understanding. They share with us opportunities presented to bring to light the layers of life events and connect to the essence of the real self.

Some of the stories in this book are about people I work with through hypnosis or shamanism. For their privacy, I have changed many of names in the book. This book is written deliberately to communicate to your subconscious mind. Please realize the formatting is purposeful to carry out this intention.

2
My Story

As in most people's stories, some events in my life have appeared to be good while others seem bad. I was one of six siblings from a large, but poor family. We were dearly loved by our parents. I told my husband today that I realized my dad was special. He gave all of his children unconditional love. By this I mean none of us had to be someone special, or act some particular way, to deserve to be loved. Dad just loved us the way we were.

Mom loved us in her special way, although she wasn't comfortable with being demonstrative like my Dad. Her actions still let us know she loved us. Mom was a nurse and a perfectionist. I can remember doing dishes - she would make us do them over again if they weren't perfectly spotless. (Actually, this is a good way to teach a child to do a job right the first time.)

We didn't spend all of our childhood doing dishes and chores; we spent a fair amount of time playing. Often, we would pack a picnic lunch and walk to the pasture to play under the old oak tree. The sun would shine through the leaves, accompanied by a nice breeze in the air.

We delighted in the feel of the grass tickling our bare feet. We would spend the day swinging in the limbs of the tree; that tree had great energy. We had lots of fun pretending we were princesses and kings who ruled the world. To this day, each of us kids fondly remembers the old oak tree.

Ours was an open house with open hearts.

There is also a dark side to my life's story which this book is about to tell. I know many of you have stories that would make mine seem insignificant. What is important about each of our stories is the way we choose to live and deal with our challenges, victories, and defeats. Connecting to your subconscious mind can help you change your story - if you choose. Many of the stories in this book are personal, exposing my soul wounds and the recovery from them.

My childhood soon moved to adulthood and at eighteen I married Steve. It was a day I remember with happiness and joy. Steve was twenty one, and as I look back at a picture of him, he looked a lot like Elvis Presley. He was six foot, four inches, weighed two hundred pounds, and was one of the best athletes in his school. What attracted me to him was his easy smile, quick sense of humor, and dancing eyes. He made me laugh and he was a good friend.

Family and friends came to help us celebrate our wedding day, and a beautiful day it was! Golden leaves were drifting down from the trees. I remember smelling fall in the air, even though the sun was shining brightly. Our wedding day was delightfully filled with laughter and fun.

To our dismay, when we arrived home from our honeymoon, there was a letter in the mail for Steve. "Greetings and salutations, you have been drafted into the United States Army." The weather turned cold, grey, and rainy. Winter had arrived and dampness settled on our happiness.

A month to the day from our wedding, Steve was shipped off to the army medical school in Texas. Next stop was Vietnam. Shortly thereafter, I found I was pregnant with our new baby, Tammy. The first two years of her life were spent away from her father. I held my breath during those years, praying that Steve would come back home to us. What was he doing? Was he safe? Every day I read in the newspaper about how many more Vietnam casualties and deaths there were. Young men were dying and my husband could be one of them. At some point, I stopped reading the papers.

Two years later, the Vietnam War ended for Steve, and he came home to us. One day he was in battle; the next day, he was a father and husband trying to figure out what to do with the rest of his life. War had irrevocably changed Steve, as memories of Vietnam had the power to resurface for him anytime, anywhere. I knew he had buried a lot. The only way I knew to help was to listen when he wanted to talk about his time on the battle field.

Sometimes, he opened up in the darkness of night, and talked about the guilt he felt. He was a medic, and questions about his decisions haunted him. Could he have done more? Was there someone he could have saved and didn't? Occasionally, he suffered from moments of flashback, memories of overturned tanks filled with screaming men. The most devastating part of those memories for Steve was the anguish and helplessness of not being able to save some of his men. To make matters worse for us, in 1966 public opinion and attitude toward Vietnam vets was hostile and mixed. I was mad! I couldn't understand how society could hate and spit on the men who defended their freedom.

Steve had not been home six months when his father, who was forty-eight years old, suddenly died of an aneurism. Steve's grief poured out for both his father and all the men he lost in war. I felt so helpless. I was grateful my dad was there to pick Steve up. He was a World War II veteran, so he understood some of the adjustments Steve was going through. He quietly offered his sympathy and support to Steve, and most of all, he helped him to remember how to have fun again and forget.

My Mom, Dad, my four younger sisters, and brother all thought Steve walked on water. All my siblings loved it when we visited the home where I grew up. Steve was always teasing and tormenting them. That gave me a warm sense of family.

Parenthood was a challenge for Steve; he didn't know quite how to relate to our two and a half year old. Of course, neither did Tammy know this tall man who was now directing her life, and she wasn't sure she trusted him. I was stuck in between. What a hard adjustment for all of us. We struggled to make a family life for ourselves, and after a while we did it. We worked hard, spent a lot of time with our large extended families, and soon we had a second baby on the way.

I laugh when I remember the differences between our two children. Tammy, our firstborn, was a beautiful little girl with bright, intelligent, inquisitive eyes, and golden-brown wavy hair down to her waist. She had a quiet sensitivity and cared about other's feelings. If you let Tammy outside to play, she was instantly covered in dirt from head to toe. She always wanted to be in the thick of things. Sometimes, her curiosity got her into trouble, like the time when she picked all our neighbor's flowers for me. Then there was the day she stuck a peanut up her nose, and we couldn't get it out. Tammy loved animals and she continually had a cat or dog following behind her. She was a very curious girl and knew how to have fun.

Our second daughter, Stephanie, two and a half years younger, had big blue eyes, and thick dark wavy hair, and was always tall for her age. The differences between the girls sometimes took me off guard. Tammy always stepped up to talk to anyone, asking lots of questions, while Stephanie always coolly appraised people. She wasn't so quick to initiate conversation. She just batted those beautiful blue eyes, set in her perfect oval face, and won people over. Stephanie was the type of baby I could take room to room, and she would be content to be near me. Tammy, on the other hand, was always exploring her boundaries, trying to see what was on the other side of the proverbial fence. Stephanie followed Tammy around everywhere, often letting her do the talking for her. Except, when Stephanie wanted her way, she got her way.

Both sides of our family were an important part of our lives. We always spent our holidays at my parent's farm. Often Steve's family came with us, which the girls absolutely loved. Every chance they got, the girls played with their cousins, just kicking around the little creek out back, catching grasshoppers and fireflies.

In 1976, an accident put Steve and me in a real struggle for our lives. We bought a new truck. We were so proud of it; we couldn't wait to show my mom and dad. We drove straight from the dealership to their house. Mom and Dad gave us all the appropriate ooh's and ah's, then we happily started on our way home. Just as we are going through a country intersection, I looked up and saw another truck barreling toward us. Instantly, I realized it was going to hit us on my side.

I screamed at Steve, "Watch out!" and ducked my head to my knees.

It was too late for Steve to avoid the accident. I heard the truck smashing into us; the impact jarred my whole body. The sound of rocks screeched on the roof as the truck rolled over and over. Intellectually, I knew the accident was happening in a few quick seconds, yet my body was experiencing it in slow motion.

After many seconds that seemed like a lifetime, the truck came to a dead stop. There was nothing but silence. I was sandwiched between the seat of the truck and the roof. I could feel my heart beating fast. My mind was struggling to grasp what had just happened. I couldn't find Steve. I kept yelling and yelling for him; he didn't answer. There was dead silence.

My head was exploding. When I put my hands on my face, I realized I couldn't feel anything except gross swelling, not even pain. I didn't know if that was a good thing or a bad thing. Then everything began to fade into blackness. The next thing I realized someone was loading both Steve and I into an ambulance. Part of me knew Steve was really hurt. Along with that our new truck had forty seven miles on it, and was totaled.

I had always wondered what it would be like to ride in an ambulance - that day I knew riding in an ambulance was horrible. Every little bump we hit jarred and sent pain through me. I could hear Steve groan every time the EMT bumped into him. It seemed like hours before we arrived at the hospital where we were taken to the emergency room, and later admitted.

My thinking was fuzzy and my face was unrecognizable. I had a severe concussion. Steve's leg had been crushed from his hip to his knee. I wasn't able see him for a day, because I was too hurt to get out of bed.

The doctor came the next day and asked if he could take me in a wheel chair to see Steve. As he wheeled me in to Steve's room, I immediately knew something was drastically wrong. Steve's color was a pasty grey. He didn't respond in any way. He was still and silent, not opening his eyes, or even recognizing me. I went back to my room praying. I knew Steve was in a fight for his life. After couple of days the doctors figured out that Steve's broken leg had thrown a blood clot which was blocking the flow of blood to his lungs and brain.

The accident changed our lives in one swift moment.

Steve was off work for the entire next year. Depression settled around him like a dark cloud. Having only the money I was making coming in to our household was stressful. Steve was such an active man before the accident, now he couldn't do anything except sit. He would get grouchy and nitpicky with the kids and me. I was struggling between keeping peace in the house, and making a living for us. The kids, at that time, were nine and eleven. Having to tiptoe around Steve was stressful for them. I begged Steve to please ask the doctor for an antidepressant (at that time "real men" didn't ask for antidepressants). When he finally did ask, things around the house began to level out somewhat.

But something else had gone wrong during that time. Not until years later, when I was sorting through old pictures, did I realize that all of Tammy's childhood pictures until around age eleven, showed her with a beautiful smile and shinning eyes. Her intelligence and inquisitiveness reflected out from those pictures. At some point, around this time, the pictures of her changed. It was as if a veil dropped over her face, her eyes were sad and guarded. We were so involved in Steve's fight for his life; we attributed the changes in Tammy as a response to what Steve was going through.

Tammy became withdrawn; she cried easily; sometimes she holed up in her room. I assumed the differences we were seeing in Tammy's behavior were also a result of changing hormones. I began to have a nagging feeling about Tammy, but I couldn't quite put my finger on it. I was worried about Steve; I was worried about the kids; and I was worried about trying to support the household. Stress was now a part of my life.

Stress as a Dragon

When Tammy was a teenager, I woke up and realized that stress was the dragon that had its claws in me, and I had no idea how to get out of its clutches. Looking back, it seemed like the dragon had crept up on us at the time of the truck accident. I felt something was not quite right with Tammy, but I'll be darned if I knew what it was. Stress had chronically entered my life with all the life changes. There was no energy left to deal with the dragon.

Most people don't realize the insidious effects stress has on your soul. Stress attracts more stress. It cripples the soul; and when it embeds in the body, it saps life force energy. Stress causes a shift from authenticity, producing more stress perpetuating a circular cycle of stress. Anything a person engages in over and over again will grow in size. So it is with stress. Before you know it, you are locked in the dragon's clutches and can't get free.

I felt like I was disappearing in all the worry. The dragon was in the room to stay, and it had me backed into a corner. I was desperate to get out of that room and into a safe place.

Given the circumstances, I couldn't find my way out of the room. When Tammy was a freshman in high school, someone told me she was smoking pot under the tree in the schoolyard with her friends. Honestly, we had never been exposed to drugs and didn't realize they were eventually going to be a major issue. Innocence/ignorance is sometimes dangerous. Tammy was stepping in poisoned water.

Steve and I confronted Tammy about her smoking pot; she denied everything. We wondered if this was a passing phase. Many kids experiment during teen years. We had no rulebook on raising a teen. We felt we could not call the school - everything was based on hearsay, and we didn't have proof that what we heard was true. How naïve we were at the time.

One day, Tammy didn't come home from school. We called all her friends, but had no luck finding her. Both Steve and I were trying to maintain a cool head, but it was a very scary feeling not knowing where our fifteen year old child was. After an excruciating few days, she called my youngest sister, Nancy. My sister talked her into calling us, and finally Tammy came waltzing through the door. I was both mad at her, and relieved that she was home and safe.

Talking to Tammy was like talking to a brick wall; all we got were evasive answers about where she was and why she left. There seemed to be two Tammy's. One who loved us, was hurting, and was sorry for hurting us. Then, there was the other Tammy who had no guilt about lying to us. She didn't seem to care about the negative consequences she was creating in both her life and ours. We had no idea what was going on, but suspected drugs were part of the problem. We entered therapy as a family, with hope in our hearts.

One evening when Steve and I were watching television in the living room, we suddenly heard "bam" and our whole house shook. Steve ran outside to see what was happening. As Tammy was pulling into the garage, she ran into the corner of the entrance. Steve told me he was pretty sure Tammy was high. Once again, we confronted her; and again, all we got was denial. We just couldn't seem to pierce the armor that Tammy had put up around herself.

Several months later, Tammy was driving home from her after school job and ran off the road, totaling her car. Steve and I grounded Tammy and didn't replace the car. We both suspected she was high when the accident happened; again we confronted her with our suspicions. As usual, she denied everything. Steve and I were extremely frustrated because we knew she was lying. Stress was now a permanent part of our lives. Where were all those lies coming from?

Tammy was smart and did well in school. She was involved in the pom-pom squad and had lots of friends. Her high school started a program in which some students could attend regular classes, while at the same time, receive vocational training. Tammy enrolled in the practical nursing course. She attended half days at high school, and afternoons at vocational school. She loved her nursing classes.

One day, I received a phone call from high school asking me what was wrong with Tammy. Apparently, someone who had identified themselves as me had called in every morning for three weeks to say Tammy was sick. Tammy kept attending vocational school in the afternoons, but was skipping high school in the morning. Who was calling in for her?

The next day Steve and I rolled out of bed determined to find answers. We followed Tammy as she got on the school bus. Arriving at school, she got off the bus and into a car with a bunch of kids. They drove to a house not far from school and went in.

Steve and I went up to the door, knocked, and asked for Tammy. The boy who answered lied, saying she wasn't there. Steve told him that unless he wanted the police at his door, he'd better bring her out to us. Tammy came to the door higher than a kite. We asked her to come with us. She just stood there with a belligerent look on her face. Steve told her that if she didn't want all the kids to be arrested in the house, she'd better quietly come along. Out she came, surly and mad. Too bad, we were mad, too.

We were still operating under the delusion that we could control Tammy's behavior.

I was in a struggle; some days were like any normal home with teenagers. Other days were shear frustration with Tammy's behavior. I was being emotionally pulled back and forth like a yo-yo. I couldn't find balance in my life.

Throughout the girl's high school years, our house was the place where both of the girls' friends came to hang out. We enjoyed all the kids, and became close to some of them. We had a ski boat. Often Steve and I took Tammy, Stephanie, and some of their friends skiing for the day. The happy family time gave us the illusion that we were living "normal lives." We cherished those moments.

Contrasting those good times, at home Tammy and I were in a struggle of wills - she was determined to drop out of school; I was determined she was going to finish. Along with that, I was disgusted by many of the choices she was making. Tammy had been kicked out of school for skipping for three weeks. I went to talk the principal about getting Tammy back into school, and he decided to accept her. She seemed to be happy to be back that first day, and I felt good that she was in school again.

The first day back, I drove her to school and went in with her. The principle welcomed her back and treated her graciously. A few hours after I dropped her off, I received a phone call from the school principal asking if I had any idea were Tammy was. She checked into the office that morning, and then blew off school. I had no a clue where to find her. As the day went on, I got madder and madder knowing she would show up back at home acting like she had gone to school.

I wasn't surprised when that afternoon she came strolling through the door acting as if she'd gone to school. I asked, "How did school go today, Tammy?" "Great, Mom," she said. I hated her looking me in the face and lying to me. I told her I knew she didn't go to school, and I would quit my job and go to school with her every day, if that's what it took to keep her there. She knew I meant it, I was determined she was going to finish school. Things leveled out with school; however, I knew she was still smoking pot. I was also concerned that she had graduated to using other drugs; I was about to find the answer.

One Smoke, No Pain

~Sharron Magyar

Who is this teenager who stops just to hide her body?
Hoping she's invisible, feeling all alone and out of grace?
Maybe one smoke will make her feel pretty,

Or at least make her not care.
What have we done so wrong to make her feel such pain?
We'll get help, a counselor should do.
What a despicable place.
We all walk in; each knowing what's wrong
Is our entire fault.
But what is really wrong? I'll be damned if I know.
I have that feeling in my gut.
It tells me something is hiding in the dark.
What could it be? It turns in my mind night after night.
Not an answer, to help in this fight, just anxiety lurking.
Outside our door, questions and illusive answers.
And then one day I realize something is out of place.
I search and search, what could it be?
For me, just an intuition,
Gnawing in my subconscious mind,
Not quite in the open, yet won't go away.

I am not sure how we ever managed to stick it out through Tammy's high school years. I breathed a sigh of relief and congratulated myself when she graduated from high school as well as vocational school. She was now a licensed practical nurse who loved nursing. Her patients loved her. She was kindhearted and knowledgeable and she took good care of her patients.

What irony, Tammy took good care of her patients, but she couldn't seem to take good care of herself. I kept asking myself why she was unable to feel self-value. Was it because she was always self-conscious about her body? She did mature earlier than most girls in her class. Tammy always felt she was overweight, even though she wasn't. Her reactions to life seemed out of proportion with the events.

Nothing seemed to make sense and I was stuck searching for answers. Subconsciously, I knew there was something I was missing. I kept going back to the idea that there were two Tammy's; one, the sensitive and caring nurse, and the other, determined to walk down a dark road. What always discouraged me was how good she was at lying.

The differences between Tammy and Stephanie were becoming more and more evident as they were growing up. Tammy was attractive with a solid earthiness. Stephanie was downright beautiful. It didn't matter what Stephanie was doing, she turned heads. Boys would do anything to get Stephanie's attention. Stephanie got good grades, was a cheerleader and a member of the track team. She only kept her grades up so she could cheerlead. Socially, she was always ready to take up for the underdog.

Stephanie knew a lot of what was going on with Tammy, but she kept quiet about it. She didn't want it to hurt us. She saw other kids at school doing drugs, and passed it off thinking they were all just partying. Couldn't be any harm in that, could there? On what would become a downward slide, Tammy graduated to using amphetamines her senior year at high school. Steve and I were clueless about the amphetamines.

The struggle to keep Tammy in school had taken its toll on me. I began to recognize I needed to do some things to keep my sense of self. I kept wondering what Steve and I had done so wrong that we deserved a life like this? I knew in my heart that God was watching over us, and that I could trust Him to bring us some good. I kept waiting for the good.

The question was, "how could I help myself?" I started exercising for stress relief; that helped quite a bit. I also enrolled in a couple of courses each semester at our local community college. I loved learning, and discovered I was a gifted artist. School kept me occupied, so that all the drama Tammy was forcing on me didn't suck me into the dark abyss. I proactively sought ways to keep my stress level down, since every day Tammy would somehow create a new drama.

After graduation, Tammy started staying out all night, coming and going as she pleased. I couldn't sleep. I knew I wouldn't set foot in the places she was going. It was strange, if we asked her to do something; she looked us in the face, agreed with us, and did what we asked. She lived a different life when she left our house. She tried to hide it from us. We knew the things she wanted were leading her to trouble.

At wits end, we asked Tammy to move out of our house. Neither Steve nor I could live with the stress she was creating at home. After she moved out, she frequently called. We saw her; we talked to her; and we enjoyed being around her. That really sweet, cool Tammy brought herself to our door. I was still aware of the other Tammy driving her life. We kept silent.

I felt so helpless, I wouldn't allow myself to feel the sadness I felt about my dear Tammy.

One day, Tammy called and told me she was pregnant. She was going to marry the father, Raymond Brown. I had known this boy all of his life, and I knew he came from a hard childhood. And although I did feel sympathy for him, I did not want Tammy to marry him. We tried to talk her out of marrying Raymond because he lived such a hard lifestyle. I liked him, he was personable, but his background made me extremely concerned.

Tammy married Raymond anyway, and into our lives came our first grandson, Stephen Ray. In looks, he reminded me of my father. He had curly hair with a stocky build. He was cute, smart and curious – so much like Tammy.

It didn't take long for things to fall apart with Tammy and Raymond. When Stephen Ray was four months old, Tammy divorced Raymond. She and the baby moved home with us. I loved children, especially this one. The baby and I developed a close bond. Steve and I played with Stephen Ray. All the while, I suspected Tammy was still using drugs, but I couldn't prove it.

One weekend, Steve and I went camping. The day after we got home, Steve went to Hardy's to have coffee with the neighborhood men. Right away, they asked him why the emergency squad was at our house over the weekend. Steve didn't know how to answer them, but he sure was going to find out. When he questioned Tammy, she told him she fell in the pool, hit her head, and was pulled out by her friends. They called 911.

Stephanie later told us, Tammy was all drugged up when she fell into the pool. Apparently, Stephanie came home to find the emergency squad at our house. She was angry, embarrassed and disgusted.

Another incident occurred around the same time, when the girls went to my sisters to swim in her pool. As soon as they got there, they fixed themselves a soda and went out to lounge around the pool. Stephanie saw Tammy swallow a handful of drugs. Soon she began slurring her words so badly that Stephanie couldn't make out what she was saying.

After a short while, Tammy excused herself and stumbled inside the house toward the bathroom. She was gone so long that Stephanie became concerned, and went to check on her. At that moment, she was weaving her way down the hall about to take another handful of drugs. Stephanie was so mad she wanted to leave, but instead she stayed for fear Tammy would drown in the pool. She called my sister to come home.

At that point in time, Stephanie knew more specifics about what was really going on with Tammy's drug abuse than we did. She kept silent. She thought there wasn't anything we could do, and she was afraid that it would break our hearts if we knew the truth. We knew the truth, Tammy was a drug addict, and we felt helpless to help her.

Tammy soon met someone new, eventually married and had two children. Amber, their first daughter, was born on a cold winter's day in January. What a beautiful surprise. She had the reddest hair, and a perfect doll shaped face. Soon to follow was Morgan, a near carbon copy of Amber, also with pretty red hair. Tammy loved the babies and treated them well. While Tammy's husband was going to radiology school, she was working at the local hospital as a nurse.

Steve and I bought a house for Tammy and her family to live in. It wasn't much of a house, but it would work until her husband finished school, and they could afford to support themselves and the children. He graduated after two years, and got a job in the radiology department at the hospital where he attended. Steve and I breathed a sigh of relief; we knew they could financially support themselves, at last. In the meantime, Tammy was being sucked further into addiction. Often, she would go to the hospital with a migraine headache. I knew she had migraines, but I suspected she was also seeking drugs.

One day, Tammy came home and told us she was fired from the hospital for stealing drugs. Tammy's life was deteriorating. Her house was a mess. She was five foot seven and her weight had dropped to about one hundred pounds. She looked emaciated, and her hands shook all the time. Tammy was physically falling apart due to her drug abuse. She didn't use street drugs. Because she was a nurse, she knew how to manipulate drugs from doctors.

At times, Steve and I would have simply walked away from it all, but we knew we couldn't abandon our grandchildren, or our daughter. Sadly we no longer felt we had a life of our own. To say the least, we were frustrated. Our life was dominated by Tammy's addiction, but we didn't know how to get off the merry-go-round we were on.

Financially, Steve and I were tapped out between the cost of years of therapy, and essentially supporting two households. I spent a lot of time balancing work, school, and taking care of my grandchildren. We prayed for help from God to know the best course of action for Tammy, and our grandchildren.

Choices

~Sharron Magyar

The choices we make often bring us pain,
Slap us in the face, we have to do it all over again.
Our fears we create in life's reality,
Trust we forget to let God be in charge.
Falling on our face like a child skinning our knee.
Crying with pain because we stumbled again,
Habits so hard to break, turning in our brain.
Taking us back to that ugly place again, longing for drugs,
Lonesome for the streets, isolated in our agony,

Taking one hit to self-destruction,
Just once, to ease a little pain.
Always an excuse taking me down that road of suffering again,
One time, one time, one time again and again;
An addict's song in his head.
That's not me I see in the mirror,
Swollen face, bloodshot eyes, shaking hands,
Stinking breath of someone else's fate,
Stealing my soul leaving me this fate, just one more time.
Your choice is to pick it up again,
Knowing full well this could be the end,
Ignoring the consequences, enjoying the pain,
A comfortable place, an excuse to do drugs again
Chasing the illusion, clearly with delusion.
Shame hidden well, in a dark place from others,
While you visit this place.
All the while you drag others into your gutter,
Sending out a shutter into the Universe.
While you satisfy that which you know one day will have to pay,
But in the figuring of the cost, you forgot the rest of us get lost,
In our tears of shame, disappointment and pain,
Because love wasn't enough
To stop the pain of your craving,
To prevent you from picking it up again, one more time.

One day Tammy got high and wrecked another car. That day her world went tumbling down around her, and she finally had to look at the life she was living. Steve and I talked and talked and talked to Tammy. She was convinced that going into drug rehabilitation would be the best for her and the kids. Steve took her to the drug rehab facility; I just didn't have the heart to do it. Steve cried all the way home. I was so sad - for him, for my daughter, for our grandchildren, and for myself.

Along with the feelings of sadness was hope that Tammy could get the help that she needed, at long last.

My grandson, Stephen Ray, came to live with Steve and I, while Amber and Morgan went to live with their father and his parents. Tammy's husband delivered divorce papers to her while she was in rehab. Mentally and emotionally, Tammy was devastated. She was trying to get off drugs while dealing with fears of losing her marriage and children. She didn't know what her future held. She could no longer avoid the guilt she felt about the mess she had created for both herself and her children.

On the home front, my husband and I were trying to provide some stability for her children. We were heartbroken. I couldn't bear to let myself think about Tammy and the kids too much. I kept asking myself, "What we did do that was so bad?" I didn't feel we deserved to live life with drama every day. As always, I held on to God, my family, and my friends as tightly as I could to get through everything. I was determined, more than ever, that I was going to finish college - it was my lifeline to normalcy.

After rehab, I was hopeful Tammy could successfully quit abusing drugs. She worked her program hard, went to AA meetings, and met new people. As Tammy's addiction progressed, she had become more and more isolated, dropping all her friendships. I knew she was lonely, fragile, and now had little support. No wonder addicts have a hard time staying off of drugs. Not only do they have to deal with the addictive components, but they have to try to pick up the pieces of their destroyed lives. It's so much all at once.

I worried about Amber and Morgan who lived with their dad and his parents. Tammy, Stephen Ray, Steve and I missed them terribly. They had never been away from us.

Time Stands Still

One day I received a phone call from my friend, Ercille, which went like this: "Sharron has anyone gotten a hold of you? Morgan, (Tammy's second daughter who was three and a half) almost drowned." Time stopped. I couldn't wrap my mind around what she said. I was in the checkout counter at the service station, and I couldn't breathe or move. A kind woman who overheard our conversation reached out to me, asking if she could help me in any way. I told her to ask my friend, Ercille, to come and get me. The stranger stayed and prayed with me until she arrived. It seemed like an eternity.

When Ercille picked me up, she had already thought to call the hospital to find out if they had pronounced Morgan dead, or if she was alive. My mind was racing and confused. I couldn't grasp a coherent thought. Tammy was about to be released from rehabilitation; it didn't even dawn on me to call her. All I could think about was getting to the hospital fast. Oh God, I thought I would die. We couldn't find out what the situation was with Morgan; the hospital wouldn't give us information over the phone.

Steve met me at the hospital. We went into the room to see sweet Morgan. She had every tube imaginable coming out of her body. She was comatose, a pasty blue color, and it didn't look like she was breathing. I thought I was going to throw up. I knew Morgan was lingering at death's door.

Steve and I walked out of the hospital room sobbing. What a beautiful child - I couldn't bear to see my granddaughter in that hospital bed. The doctors weren't giving us much hope.

Soon every one of our family and friends showed up at the hospital. We all went to the chapel to pray. I prayed to God to save my granddaughter, saying, "Whatever is Your Will, I will accept." I knew I would have to accept her death, or her life forever changed. It would be the hardest thing I ever had to go through, no matter what. God help me, I knew no one intended to hurt my granddaughter, but they failed to protect her. I didn't know how to find forgiveness in my heart, so I set it on the shelf to work on later.

By afternoon, Tammy was able to get out of rehab to come to the hospital. She was in shock. Her grief was so deep that I didn't know if she would ever recover. Her resolve was strong; she knew she needed to hold on for Morgan. I can't put into words the agony of watching both my granddaughter and my daughter in so much pain. Though Tammy had her faults, she did love her children greatly. She held Morgan, she rocked her, and she cried and cried until there were no more tears left.

Tammy dug in; her nurses' training took over to help Morgan. She instinctually knew what to do to help relieve her child's pain. I was astonished - I was able to see firsthand her ability as a nurse. Steve, Tammy, and I were staying at the hospital around the clock. Tammy's husband and his family came in and out.

Morgan immediately and repeatedly convulsed day after day. She couldn't move or even open her eyelids. We didn't know if she could hear us talking to her. I cannot tell you what it was like to see my big bear of a husband brought to his knees knowing Morgan had almost drowned. Seeing Morgan in so much pain was excruciating.

Kindnesses were extended to us in a million ways: with a hug, people just dropping by to say "Hi, I was thinking of all of you," "How can we help you?" Sometimes they brought us food and other times they just came to sit with us. The two policemen, who did so much for Morgan in the initial moments of her near drowning, visited daily. This grandchild of mine touched so many lives. Everyone's hearts and prayers were given daily.

Love and hope kept us hanging on.

Tammy stayed drug free through it all, but we knew she was fragile. She mindfully focused on Morgan - settling into a routine of living, sleeping, and eating at the hospital.

One day, while I was at the hospital, I thought I saw Morgan move her hands and feet. Up to this point she couldn't even open her eyelids. Though the movement was uncontrolled with shakiness, I could tell her brain had begun to re-connect with her body. First it began at her fingers and toes. I could literally see it; I had no idea what this faint movement really meant for Morgan. I then saw her movement beginning to progress inward to her hands, arms, feet and legs. After three days, she had the ability to move all of her body although she couldn't control it yet. This gave us a little sliver of hope.

We held her, read to her - we treated her as if she could hear every word we spoke to her. Here is one of our favorite stories we read her:

♥ ♥ ♥

Once upon a time, there grew a very special sunflower. It was a sunflower that started to grow on very solid ground. But the wind and the rains came after it started growing, blowing it this way and that. The wind and rain was strong, unpredictable, and scary.

The flower became all mixed up about who it was and how it was supposed to grow. Rather than growing into a tall solid sunflower, it split into many different flowers, each different in maturity, age, and size. Somehow the flower split to protect itself against the storms. One part became a flower growing tall and skinny; another part of the flower was bending over, its leaves hanging low in sorrow. A third flower was like a rose filled with thorns, prickly and hurt from the split. A very young sprout grew out of the flower with a very diseased leaf, and an old hard seed.

The sunflower could not grow in the way it was intended to grow, because it was split into many different individual flowers. Parts of it were tall, parts of it were small, but mostly it was all mixed up. The other sunflowers in the garden did not understand this sunflower at all, because they had never seen a sunflower like it before. They often snickered and made fun of the sunflower because it was different.

One day, a fairy came walking through the flower garden, and stopped before the confused sun flower. The fairy got a very puzzled look on her face and said, "Gosh little flower, you somehow have gotten all mixed up. You're supposed to be a sunflower, but you have split into many different flowers. And that means you can't grow tall and straight and beautiful to feel the warmth of the sun."

The little sun flower started to cry, and the fairy was taken aback, because she didn't know sun flowers could cry. The flower sobbed, "I know I'm all mixed up." She felt terrible. The flower told the fairy, "The winds and the rains hurt me when I was little." Sometimes one part of me doesn't know what the other part is doing, and I feel confused. The sunflower asked the fairy to help her.

The fairy looked at the sunflower intensely, and then decided that maybe she had a solution. She said, "I must cut away the leaves of all the different flowers that grow from your stem. Then I'll wrap you up so that you grow into one strong healthy stem."

"How bad will it hurt me?" asked the sunflower as she was crying.

The fairy said, "It might hurt a little bit, but after it's done you will feel much, much prettier and stronger."

The little sun flower was afraid, but decided she would not let her fear keep her from growing as it had before. As carefully as she could, the fairy stripped off the funny looking leaves and then separated the stems, which grew from the sunflower. Then the fairy wrapped some silk from the spider around the flower, making sure that all the stems were close together. The fairy reassured the sunflower, "I'll be back later to take away the silk. You may soon find you are one solid sunflower again."

The sunflower felt a little strange and scared but she grew stronger and healed more and more. Sometimes, for a brief moment, she was sorry that she'd met the fairy, especially when she saw that it was going to rain and the wind was going to blow, but she wasn't unhappy for very long. Mostly, she was encouraged that all her parts could grow together as the fairy had predicted.

Before long, the fairy was back, "I'm going to remove the silk," the fairy informed the flower. Let's take a look at you."

The sunflower was happy to discover her stem was now solid, although her leaves were a little pale yellow from being covered up. This made the sunflower frightened. The fairy saw her anxiety.

"Your leaves will be healthy as soon as the sun shines on them," said the fairy." Soon you will be completely healed, and no one will remember that you were anything other than a beautiful sun flower."

The sunflower cried tears of joy, she was so delighted. "How can I thank you?" she asked.

"You can thank me by growing stronger and stronger every day. You will be the sturdiest sunflower in the garden." The sunflower grew; she flourished, standing straight and tall to shine in the sun. The fairy danced away smiling; she knew the sunflower was going to be alright.

In a month's time, Morgan's movements became fitful and jerky. Because she was hard to hold we were all physically tired and emotionally exhausted. The intellectual part of me said that I needed to videotape her progress, yet the emotional part could not muster the heart or the courage. The newspapers wanted to interview us, but none of us were able to talk with them without breaking down, so we refused interviews. What was there to say? It was an accident. We would all have to live with the outcome. Morgan, in particular, would live with it for the rest of her life.

Reflecting on the emotional toll, Tammy's drug abuse felt like a walk in the park compared to Morgan's near tragic death.

I Am In the Right Place

Morgan's recovery from her near-fatal drowning occupied most of my time. We were with Morgan in the hospital for months helping her learn to use her muscles and to speak. I have to admit, a part of me felt sorry for myself. Why me? Why do I have a daughter that's a drug addict? Why did this happen to Morgan? Why do I have to be under so much stress? After six months that seemed like years, my life settled into taking Morgan to rehab at the hospital three times a week.

I remember in particular one snowy day when we arrived at the hospital. It was difficult to get Morgan in and out of the car, because of her lack of balance. After much heaving and struggling, I got her into the stroller. The hospital was under construction with several blocked entrances. The detour was irritating. I had to keep myself from tripping in the snow, and from tipping Morgan out of the stroller.

By the time we got inside the door, I was grumpy, irritated, and stressed. The basement we were re-routed through gave me an eerie feeling. I knew this was an area closed to the general public. As we were walking by some equipment, Morgan looked over and said, "I don't like that machine, it made me hurt." I was astonished at her comment, because at the time, we didn't know if she had any conscious awareness, or not. Apparently, she did. I was reminded why I was there.

When we finally arrived at the rehab desk, the receptionist took our names and told us to take a seat. My irritation increased; we had to wait again. As I sat there, I began to get a handle on my emotions. I looked around the room and saw another woman who was so very young. Her son was about nine or ten and couldn't even hold up his head. I started a conversation with her, asking her if she had brought her son into the hospital by herself. She said she'd carried him in. I was stunned. I didn't know how she did it, as he was almost as big as she was. Then she told me her son had been ill since birth, and she was his only caretaker.

Apparently, her husband was so angry about his boy's disabilities that he refused to help the mom in any way. She had no family to help her out, either. Shame filled my face. I realized I was in the perfect place to give the mother a word of encouragement. I did not understand God's plan for me. However, I made up my mind, right then and there, to be open to it.

From my perspective, I was having a bad morning. From the mother's perspective, she was grateful to be at the hospital where she could get some help. Okay, Lord, I get the lesson - It is about giving thanks regardless of the circumstance. The biblical story of Job came to mind as a beautiful example. His thankfulness and fidelity to God was hugely rewarded after great strife. I was searching for ways to keep myself centered, balanced, and thankful through all the turmoil.

My First Hypnosis

After Morgan's near drowning, I knew I had emotionally hit a brick wall. I was in big trouble if another crisis came my way. I decided to make an appointment with a professor at college who was both a counselor and hypnotherapist. Sitting in his office, I explained that I didn't have the resources to deal with any more stressful situations. He asked me if I knew what emotion was giving me a problem. My reply was, "There are so many emotions I don't know where to start. At other times, I am emotionally tapped out." I knew he didn't have enough time in the day to listen to my story.

The counselor asked me if he could hypnotize me, and explained that sometimes hypnosis can be a good way to get in touch with feelings, and help heal them. I agreed. He began talking to me in a nice soothing voice, helping me to relax my mind and body. After I was relaxed, he again asked me if I knew what emotion was giving me trouble.

I heard myself say, "Yes, sadness." The analytical part of me was still thinking, "That's strange, I didn't even know that intellectually." He gave me the direction to let all that sadness come up so I could feel it in my body. It welled up in my stomach like a great big ball and then it rose to my throat and exploded. I cried and cried. (Wow, I sure didn't know all that was there!)

The next day I felt detached and introspective. I rolled out of bed, and I wrote about all the sadness I had denied myself. I felt a sense of relief and lightness and knew I was doing much better. Analytically, I filed away the experience and noted hypnosis can be a very powerful tool in releasing problematic emotions.

For me, hypnosis was also a stepping stone to a new awareness about the healing potential within us. Being open and receptive to a modality I was unfamiliar with had a huge personal reward for me. The counselor told me that emotions can only become problematic, when we will not allow ourselves to feel them fully, and then work through them.

Tammy's Transplant

Morgan entered into months of rehabilitation at St. Louis Cardinal Glennon Hospital. Rehabilitation therapists teamed up to work with her. In as little as an hour, they were exhausted. Day by day, therapists painstakingly taught Morgan how to walk, talk, and do all the things her body had formerly done without thinking. She mindfully focused on every task they gave her. My granddaughter had grit: she taught me the true meaning of determination and will. She was going to live, but it was going to be a long tough road to recovery. What recovery would mean for her, we didn't know.

Tammy never left the hospital except during times when Steve and I went to help her out. She was wearing down, and realized she needed support from AA. She called them, and they sent someone to pick her up and take her to the meeting. In every way, we tried to give Tammy and Morgan all the support we could.

In the meantime, Tammy still had a sliver of glass in her eye from her car accident. She scheduled an appointment with the eye clinic in St. Louis. They took the silver out, and covered her eye with a contact lens. When Tammy walked in and told me what they'd done, I got an icky feeling in my stomach. I wanted to scream, "Get it out! Get it out!" There was nothing rational about my reaction. I was dumbfounded by my emotions; however, I couldn't shake them off. I was feeling an unidentifiable unease about Tammy's eye.

The whole time she was at the hospital with Morgan, Tammy's eye was killing her. The doctor gave her special antibiotics for the eye, but they didn't help. It began to ooze a sticky brown substance. The doctor then put a patch on the eye which made her nauseated and dizzy. He kept having her come back and back again and again, but he couldn't seem to find out what was wrong with her eye.

Worrying she would lose her eye; she switched to different eye doctor at home. He bragged he knew what was wrong with Tammy's eye. He started a different course of treatment, after which, the eye oozed even more. At this point, so much medicine had been put in her eye, she became reactive to a many of the eye drugs. The new doctor recommended, and then performed a corneal transplant. Tammy's medical records showed she was addicted to drugs. In my observation, it seemed the doctor had determined she was worthless; he was rough with her and her eye.

With no eye improvement, we were desperate for help. I did some research to locate a facility specializing in difficult eye conditions. I learned of an eye clinic in Iowa City that had one of two microscopes in the United States that can be put on the eye to make a diagnosis. We scheduled an appointment for Tammy. Immediately, the doctor in Iowa diagnosed an acanthamoeba in her eye, which could have entered on a contaminated contact lens. The amoeba had literally eaten her cornea. Another corneal transplant was scheduled.

Surgery was risky for Tammy in more ways than one. We were afraid because we knew Tammy would need to take drugs. Would drugs pull her back into addiction? She got through the first surgery fine, and handled the second without going back to the drugs. Sadly, once again her body rejected the cornea and the doctors recommended another transplant.

Tammy was broken hearted; she had had such high hopes for the last surgery. The third transplant was unsuccessful also. It would be the last one - she said she couldn't go through another. The pain was relentless. She was experiencing high pressure in her eye, which made her nauseated. With the exception of removing her eye, the doctors were at a loss as to how to help her. Tammy was not ready to lose her eye.

She and her children came to live with us after Morgan was released from hospital. Our house turned into complete chaos with Tammy and the kids. Steve was going nuts! He loved the grandchildren, but the chaos conflicted with his need for order in his life. After a year, we bought a house close to us for Tammy and the kids to live in. Our new routine involved getting Morgan to rehab, Tammy to the eye doctor, and me to school.

One day, Tammy received paperwork from her ex-husband's lawyer. He had filed papers for custody of Amber and Morgan. Morgan had never been out of our sight since she'd almost drowned. Tammy got sick and went into a panic. Amber and Morgan's father won the custody battle; he took the girls away. From that point on, Steve and I rarely got to see our two granddaughters. We went to our attorney. We found out grandparents didn't have visiting rights in Illinois, at that time. Steve and I were devastated. My heart was broken: I cried a million tears for the loss of my grandchildren. Steve couldn't talk about it.

What was happening with the girls? Were they safe? I had spent almost every day of their lives with them up to that point. Out of everything we'd been through, this was the blow I could not reconcile. Tammy entered into a depression so deep and profound I didn't think she would ever return from it.

Life moved on, broken-hearted, or not.

After a year, Tammy started dating someone she met in rehab. Jeff was about five foot, seven inches, and had dark naturally wavy hair, with the darkest brown eyes that crinkled when he laughed. He was smart, and a hard worker with an awesome sense of humor. I liked Jeff a lot, but I was concerned that Tammy was taking on someone else's trouble, since he had a past history. Even though he wasn't currently drinking, I knew how hard it was to master addiction.

The next thing I knew, Tammy was pregnant by Jeff. I was livid, to say the least. *My life had turned to shit*! I loved my husband, I loved our children and grandchildren, but I felt had no control over any part of my life. I was tired of struggling. Here we were, supporting Tammy and her children, and she was bringing another child into the world. I stayed in that mad place for awhile, and then started thinking about my grandchildren. I remembered they were the best thing in my life. Being angry was useless; I shifted my attitude. Tammy loved her children and they loved her. I enjoyed every moment I spent with the grandchildren.

This was Jeff's first child, and he was thrilled to have a baby. They named their new baby girl, Cheyenne. She had large, beautiful brown eyes like her dad's. She was the most alert baby I have ever seen. I laughed because she reminded me of my mother's energy. Tammy had her hands full with her children, yet she seemed to be in tune with them.

About six months into Tammy and Jeff's relationship, Steve and I suspected Jeff was drinking again. In time, we became sure of it. When he wasn't drinking, he was articulate, a hard worker, sensitive, and kind. Even though Tammy loved Jeff, she eventually broke off her relationship with him. She felt broken by Morgan's situation, by her continuing eye condition, and by her loss of Jeff. Tammy couldn't pull herself out of the hole she was in. She went to a doctor who put her on antidepressants.

Along the way, I kept seeking relief from the stress. (Focus on the moment. Don't bite off big chunks.) I began to recognize a need to do some things to keep myself balanced and centered. When was God going to send the good to our life?

I was learning stress can be perpetuated by the way you choose to respond to the stressor. Day by day, I tried to comprehend why we were living this life. Eventually, I was able to find the courage to ask what life expected of me.

3
Limitless Mind

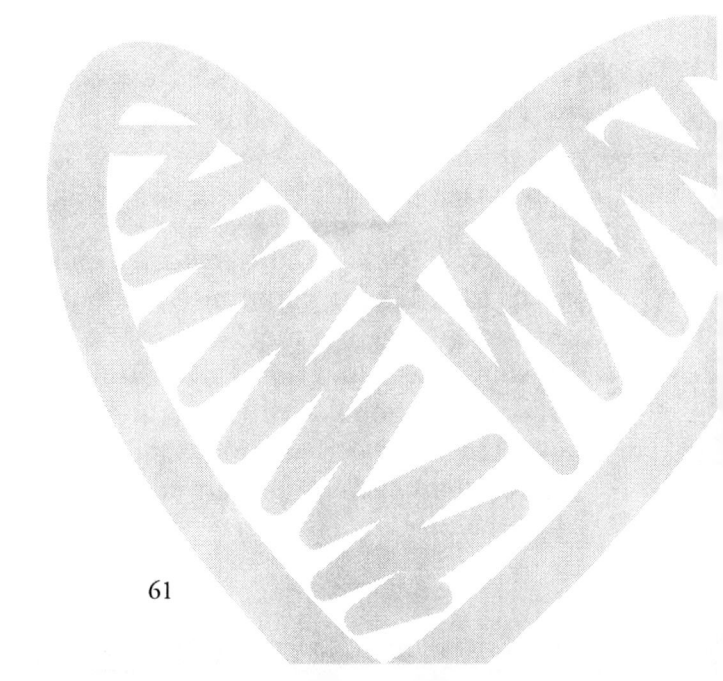

Like most people, I like to think of myself as a conscious being having control over my thoughts, feelings, and behavior. I especially want to think that I control my life. The older and more experienced I get, the more awareness I have of the fact that our lives are driven by both the conscious and subconscious mind.

The conscious mind holds sensations, perceptions, memories, feelings, and fantasies *inside* of our current awareness. It is centered on mental processing - thinking logically and talking rationally. The conscious mind maintains control by analyzing and making judgments about what is right or wrong. It has limited processing capacity, and can handle just a few tasks at a time.

Life events hit the conscious mind first. If thoughts and feelings are overwhelming, they may filter down to the subconscious mind. The subconscious mind is not limited by the conscious mind, and has an autonomy all its own.

Subconscious Mind

The term subconscious refers to any part of the mind *outside* of conscious awareness. The functionality of the subconscious is magnificent.

Often I think of the subconscious as a computer with many files. Like any computer, the subconscious handles and processes huge amounts of information at one time and is a master at multi functioning. As humans, our computer system (or subconscious) is filled with information which can be accessed by selectively focusing inward. Your subconscious does not analyze or judge, yet contains emotions which can dictate your life.

The subconscious mind has safety features for the mind and body. It safeguards against shocks and wounds. It also protects our bodies from overloading us with negative emotions and experiences which we may not be emotionally prepared to process. Each of us carries experiences, beliefs, and words so painful that we push them out of our conscious awareness, and into our subconscious mind.

Our subconscious contains many files. One file in the subconscious computer system is connected with the automatic body functions such as control of your beating heart, nervous system and various organs. All bodily urges, such as hunger and thirst are directed from the subconscious mind. Instincts such as self-protection and sex also originate on the subconscious level. The subconscious mind runs this system the best it can until your death, unless it becomes infected with the virus of illness.

Another file in your subconscious is a record of everything that has happened to you through past lives as well as your current life. This includes all events from the moment of your conception. The function of remembering involves moving data from our subconscious mind to our conscious mind. The conscious mind is selective, with a limited capacity to what and how much it can remember one time. Without our subconscious memory file, both thinking and learning would be out of the question. Much information which is stored in this file is out of our conscious awareness.

Psychological processes such as denial, introjections, projection, and intuition are beyond conscious awareness and reside inside one file in the subconscious. Because of this, sometimes, we are not consciously aware of our actions; the program is simply being run. Nearly all our emotions happen in the moment without our being aware of "why." It is as we later examine them, we are able to evaluate why we acted in a specific way.

Like any large computer system, your subconscious simply takes directions and follows those directions until it is given new programming. It never analyses why it is doing something unless it is directed to do so. With the subconscious, you can give it new directions by simply re-programming it with a different set of suggestions.

Unfortunately, similar to a computer, our subconscious can be infected with virus. Our viruses are dysfunctional habits and beliefs. It is a simple matter to rewrite a new program with more efficient programs for old habits and beliefs by using hypnosis. The role of the subconscious mind is much larger than many recognize and is brilliant in its functionality.

Superconscious Mind

The superconscious mind is connected with a higher level of consciousness called the universal consciousness or quantum consciousness. It is the source of all power, knowledge, love and peace. The superconscious knows no time or space has no limitations and is the source of all miracles.

Connecting with your superconscious is often referred to de-hypnosis in that you de-hypnotize yourself from restrictive beliefs you accepted about yourself and your relationship with the world.

Michael Persinger in the video, "No more Secrets", notes that universal information is available to all of us through geo magnetic fields. Some people believe this level of mind interacts with the brain and human energy field, yet is not actually part of the brain or body. If you want to invent or create something new, and you don't have the knowledge to do it, you can access this higher level of mind to get information. Psychics naturally connect with the geo magnetic field to gather information, yet this ability is available to all of us with proper access.

It is commonly believed to access the superconscious you must get past the subconscious. When you align the conscious with the subconscious as well as the superconscious you will naturally attract what you want to appear in your life. You think a thought and the next moment it manifests. Meditation, hypnosis and brainwave training are tools that can help you access the superconscious levels of mind.

Hypnosis

Most people think of hypnosis as being extraordinary. Milton Erickson was wise enough to recognize that it is so ordinary, that you go in and out of hypnosis on a regular basis every day.

Have you ever driven somewhere and not remember passing familiar landmarks until after you arrived? While your conscious mind was focusing on something else, your subconscious mind did the driving. Were you ever so into a book, television show, or video game that you were unaware of what was going on around you? These are examples of how we naturally enter hypnosis in our daily lives.

Hypnosis is a keen state of focus and concentration which induces a suggestible state of mind. When you are hypnotized, you understand instructions in an uncritical, automated fashion. Personal memory and awareness can be altered by suggestions given during hypnosis, which then influence your actions and beliefs in your daily world.

You do have free will in accepting or rejecting hypnotic suggestions.

Hypnosis has a specific characteristic of time distortion we call trance, similar to daydreaming. Learning in an "altered time state" can allow you to familiarize yourself with new knowledge in a smaller amount of time. Children are experts at going in and out of hypnosis as a normal function. They often use the above mentioned time phenomenon for rapidly absorbing information. Also, when a child daydreams, they use self-hypnosis to naturally practice future actions. What most people don't realize is the phenomenon of hypnosis can be engaged upon demand, to enhance learning and make changes in behavior.

Imagine that you are a football player. Now imagine in full and vivid detail making a touchdown. Make it as real in your mind as if you are physically there. See the ball; feel it in your hands, hear the cheering, notice the motion and feel of your body. Visualizing the touchdown scripts the subconscious for positive actions the next time you want to make a touchdown. Also, the subconscious does not distinguish a difference between imagining or physically making a touchdown.

In the book, *Psycho Cybernetics,* Maxwell Maltz notes that experiential and clinical psychologists have recognized, beyond a doubt, the brain is not adept at distinguishing between genuine experience and one imagined in full and vivid detail.

A consulting hypnotist is an expert in helping you to focus your attention. This selectively focused attention helps you to be open to accepting suggestions.

When a hypnotist asks you to close your eyes, they move your attention toward an inner state, in order to connect you with knowledge and procedures for problem solving. Body relaxation, combined with closing your eyes and breathing deeply, initiates changes in the brain waves linked with creative awareness, feeling and imagistic understanding. During hypnosis, the brain switches to a more holistic processing which takes place in an "out of time" orientation, offering enormous potential for emotional and physical changes.

Many people use self-hypnosis to deepen their use of self suggestion. Often, people think of using self-hypnosis for deep relaxation to eliminate stress. Scientifically documented studies have produced an extensive list of conditions that self-hypnosis can benefit. They include helping alleviate problems such as: chronic pain, headaches, muscle tension, chronic fatigue, irritable bowel syndrome, and insomnia.

The applications of self-hypnosis are as vast as your creativity to set goals for yourself. Basic induction with self-hypnosis should be practiced once a day. The duration over which you see change may be immediate, or can take up to twenty-one days. Consistency is important with self-hypnosis.

Soul Exercise # 2: Self-Hypnosis

Crafting the Suggestions:

Adapt the basic induction for your personal goals by adding specific hypnotic suggestions.

Always do self-hypnosis in a quiet, private place. Suggestions should be:

- ♥ Simple
- ♥ Positive
- ♥ Believable
- ♥ Stated in the present
- ♥ Measurable
- ♥ Carry a reward
- ♥ Written out in advance

Be sure to imagine the emotion or sensation of the goal you wish to achieve. Picture it as though it is already occurring.

Self-Hypnosis Instructions

Self-suggestion, concentration and imagination are the tools you use for self-hypnosis. It is important to avoid the analytical approach; this keeps your conscious mind alert. Remember to find a comfortable place to be alone. There are many methods for inducing self-hypnosis; the following is a quick, easy one. Don't make it complicated!

Carefully craft your suggestion before entering your induction. Write your positive suggestion on a 3X5 card which you can carry with you at all times. Focus your mind on a positive statement while in a relaxed state. You will experience a high level of focus and concentration in self-hypnosis. This state of mind will help you generate important changes in order to reach your goals.

Do the exercise at least once a day - if possible, twice a day. You will soon find yourself making permanent changes that impact your life in a positive way.

- 💜 The process takes approximately twenty to thirty minutes. The time it takes will become shorter when you become more practiced.

- 💜 To avoid falling asleep, sit up; do not lie down.

Begin Self-Hypnosis:

Close your eyes and slowly release your mind of any thought or emotion. It takes practice. Don't get discouraged if thoughts intrude, just observe them and let them go. Let your thoughts take their own direction . . . . Contract and release every muscle from head to toe, and let the stress and tension flow away from your body. Check in with your body to see where you are still holding tension. If so, contract and release the muscles in that area again.

Take a deep breath. Breathe deeply into your belly for seven counts; hold your breath for seven counts; exhale for seven counts, and hold for seven counts. Repeat this process seven times. Breathe in tranquility and peace as you inhale. Breathe out stress and tension as you exhale. Through repetition you will step into a natural breathing rhythm.

When you are fully relaxed use your imagination and visualize yourself happy and in a safe place. Engage your senses - what do you smell? hear? feel? taste? and see? Step deeper into the sensory experience and intensify it.

Imagine you are at the top of a staircase and you are descending. There are 10 steps to go down, and as you go down the steps, say to yourself, "deeper". When you reach the bottom, you should be completely relaxed and in a deep state of hypnosis. It may take fifteen to twenty minutes for beginners to totally relax.

Choose a spot on the wall in front of you, slightly above eye-level, and hold the suggestion card in front of the spot. Read the suggestion to yourself three times. Make sure the words on the card are believable to you. You may put the card down and close your eyes again. Allow yourself to imagine accomplishing what is written on the card, while repeating the suggestion over and over in your mind. Use your vivid imagination. Eventually, the suggestion may begin breaking up, while you only capture pieces of the words. That is okay. Allow yourself to simply be in the space.

After you feel complete with the process, start counting 1, 2, 3, 4, and 5. At the end of counting, you will awaken refreshed and in a normal state of consciousness. Open your eyes after a few moments and slowly get up.

The whole process is aimed at self-improvement. For your benefit and success, give yourself time for the suggestion to take hold.

Metaphors

The Indian tribe gathers around the fire in the darkness of the night. The stars are twinkling brightly, shining down on the tribe as they have for millions of years. Firelight glows softly on each face. Shadows dance in and out. Anticipation is huge as the elder begins to tell the age old stories about the heritage of the tribe, and the challenges it has faced across the ages. Each member of the tribe becomes mesmerized as the elder conveys the mysteries and connects the tribes past, present and future.

Metaphors are a wonderful way of telling stories that can make positive changes and learning. Metaphorical stories have been used for many generations as a primary method of both teaching and passing information from generation to generation. They speak to the subconscious with the comparison of two unlike things which helps us to understand the unknown.

The most commonly used example of metaphor is "He is the apple of my eye" or "He has a heart of stone." Everyday language is often interspersed with metaphors because they are a faster way to convey information. Metaphors use an "ambiguous language" which allows the listener the opportunity to add their own interpretation to the story.

In the previous discussion about the subconscious mind, I used a metaphor likening the subconscious to a computer. This instantly creates pictures in your mind of the functionality of the subconscious. You filled in the details about the computer with your individual memories and experiences.

Metaphorical stories reach across many religions and cultures. The Bible, the Kabbalah, and the Koans of Zen, use metaphors as their favorite mode of teaching. Religions transfer a wealth of metaphors in parables. Native Americans, Aborigines, the Chinese, and other indigenous cultures also use metaphors to pass along their cultural heritage. Traditions have been passed on for thousands of years through the language of metaphors.

Noted psychiatrist, such as Carl Jung and Milton Ericson, realized the significance of metaphors. Carl Jung emphasized the importance of symbols and their connections to archetypes such as: mother/father, masculine/feminine, inner child/adult, God/devil, and trickster/hero. He knew that metaphors use signs and symbols to convey information for personal transformation and individuation. Jung noted that symbols are efficient in communicating to the subconscious.

Like Jung, Milton Ericson realized the importance of metaphorical stories. In *My Voice Will Go with You*, Rosen shared tales that Ericson used for much of his psychotherapy work. When working with his clients, students, and audiences, Ericson used in his "teaching talks" which are short metaphorical stories. (Rosen, 1982)

Metaphors are interactive. They bypass resistance and encourage the imagination. The consulting hypnotist makes a conscious choice to carefully use words that will elicit a desired response. Words that contain certain vagueness allow the client to fill in the gaps with their creative imagination. Hypnotists often use metaphors with the client to provide assistance in developing problem solving and decision making skills, without the client having to decide consciously whether to accept or reject a suggestion.

Time and Space

Quantum science has proven that energy is the basis of our material existence. Can you imagine everything forming one large piece of energy? Attention and intention create an object, while spirit and intelligence accumulate energy into form. It is accepted by science that energy is powered by intelligence and communicates across space and time.

Quantum physics applies to the Universe, and likewise applies to your subconscious mind. The subconscious is not locked into traditional or linear time like the conscious mind . . . . and finds linear time to be of no importance. The subconscious mind can easily expand or contract time according to individual needs. These changes happen only when our conscious control has significantly relaxed. Time often passes slowly – or stops altogether – in moments of crisis or even in moments of creative flow. The Aborigines call the subconscious suspension of time "great time." Shamans call time suspension "the other world."

When you can drop all thoughts, time disappears. Mihally Csikszentmihaliyi in the book, *Flow: the Psychology of Optimal Experience*, explains that the flow experience makes time stand still. Csikszentmihaliy tells us the pressure of passing time is relieved if you are truly living and enjoying yourself in the moment. In the flow, awareness and understanding of time stops, allowing spirit to take over.

Albert Einstein once explained relativity to a layman by telling him, "Time passes differently for an observer when a beautiful woman rests her hand on your leg." Einstein once explained Relativity for a layman by telling him. Because time is a construct made by man, it cannot be controlled.

Time is a construct invented by man, but what is the meaning of this to individuals? On a conscious level we need to hold onto our idea of time to feel safe and secure, seeking happiness. True meaning and happiness is created through activity in which we create a sense of self. We can set the foundation for rapid learning and transformation by understanding the compression or expansion of time available in the subconscious mind.

> Each of us can manifest the properties of a field of consciousness that transcends space, time, and linear causality.
>
> ~ *Stanislaw Grof*

Milton H. Erickson

A new client gingerly opened the door to peek his head into my office at Golden Heart Hypnosis. I didn't know what his expectations were. Perhaps he expected to see voodoo heads hanging from the ceiling. One thing for sure, I could tell he was still operating under the belief that I was going to make him bark like a dog, cluck like a chicken, and stand on his head for fifteen minutes. Maybe he thought I would make him rob a bank, too. Sounds silly, but the point is he had what I call TV misperception. He thought I could *make* him act out anything with hypnosis without having a choice in the matter. It made me chuckle - in reality I knew better.

If a person still believes old wives' tales about hypnosis, and is still willing to make an appointment anyway, I assume he is motivated to make changes. The client who was peering in the door had some erroneous beliefs, so my first job was to educate him about what hypnosis is and isn't. The fact is, under hypnosis, you are in full control of yourself and aware of your environment. Hypnosis cannot make you say or do anything that you morally or ethically object to. He had a fear of being left in a hypnotized state and never waking up. Hypnosis is not sleep.

If you are hypnotized and the hypnotist leaves the room you will come out of hypnosis in a short time on your own, or you may actually fall asleep and awaken later. I spent some time with my client and explained that while experiencing hypnosis you have a greater awareness than when you are fully awake, and you completely retain your powers of selectivity which means - he didn't have to worry about my discovering his secrets either. Before we started our work, I also let him know that hypnosis does not cure everything.

Hypnosis is very safe and natural. It can help improve your life and general well-being.

Over the years, I have learned a considerable amount from the work of Milton Erickson. He had a unique approach to what he considered the correct use of hypnosis. He believed in honoring the client by establishing a rapport and he emphasized that success can be achieved through a permissive, accommodating, and indirect approach.

In my work I use Erickson style; it is permissive, in that the client takes an active role in the hypnosis process. It is accommodating, in that I utilize whatever the client presents, and work within the client's framework. It is indirect, in that I use the client's own intuitive means of accomplishing goals, without the imposition of direct suggestion. (Direct suggestion can sometimes be indicative of the hypnotherapist's restricted view of how goals should be met.)

My method gives the client the opportunity to choose, accept, or reject suggestions at their own pace, in their own time, and to allow their subconscious mind to help them achieve their goals. What a beautiful heritage Erickson passed to hypnotists today. My commitment is to give honor to Milton Erickson's wisdom every day that I work with hypnosis.

Trance and the Role of Ritual

The drumming is insistent and persistent. Waves enter the center of my body; I feel relaxation spread throughout. A shift takes place. I am confused, and then I drop into a still place; I am floating and drifting, content just to be. I am.

I recently returned from a wonderful experience at a shamanic workshop. Since my orientation is in hypnosis, I was interested in comparing the two modalities. I learned that shamanism utilizes the following:

- Drumming
- Ritual
- Chanting
- Dance
- Trance

Ritual can help you raise your own energetic vibrations by providing a safe outlet for hurtful emotions to be expressed. Shamanism uses rituals to:

- Heal
- Gain information.
- Solve problems.
- Honor and celebrate nature, seasons, and earth.
- To meet and improve your relationship with your power animals.

Sometimes rituals are personal. You can use them to solidify intentions, and confirm new actions, roles, and behaviors for your subconscious mind to adopt. Using ritual in your physical world that corresponds with your internal experience gives you a method of imprinting that experience on the subconscious mind. Some rituals involve rites of passage, to mark moving from one phase of life to another.

Often ritual can help you to identify with the sacred, making an impact at a primal level. Connecting to the miraculous and the mysterious aspects of ritual can be life changing.

Soul Exercise # 3: The Eagle

Always do meditation in a relaxing, private place. You may tape record this meditation and play it back.

Take a deep breath. Inhale deeply into your belly for seven counts; hold your breath for seven counts; exhale for seven counts, and hold for seven counts. Repeat this process seven times. Breathe in tranquility and peace as you inhale. Breathe out stress and tension as you exhale. Eventually, you will step into a natural breathing rhythm and fall into a deep relaxation.

- Imagine you see the eagle sweep down and land. You climb up on his back. He rises into the air, higher and higher into the sky. You feel the wind against your face and the sun soaking into your skin. Stress leaves your body.

- The more you soar upon the wind, the freer you become of all worries and strain. You look down upon the earth and you become connected with the universe. You realize those things you spend your days worrying about are really nothing except your imagination at play.

♥ You breathe the air into your body and hold it deep in your belly. Then you exhale, and with each out breath you exhale stress. You are free!

♥ When your body has released all stress, you and your eagle return to the earth. You breathe peace into your body. When you have returned home you count to five and open your eyes to reorient into the room

> When you align yourself with your higher self and your life purpose, miraculous things happen.
>
> ~Wayne Dyer

4
Life Lessons From Houdini

> The greatest discovery of my generation is that a human being can alter his life by altering his attitude.
>
> ~William James

While my sister was gallivanting on a yacht in the Caribbean, I was babysitting her dog, Houdini. Are you noting a hint of jealousy? Houdini is very special pitbull. He is lovable, curious, and extremely smart. He can get out of any fence, hence his name, Houdini. Usually, my husband Steve and Houdini are sidekicks, but Houdini and I were on our own for a few days.

It was a beautiful sunny day in Illinois. Fifty degrees in January (a rarity) so I decided to take Houdini to a wildlife sanctuary. Going for a walk was a brave thing for me. As a result of getting hit by a car I couldn't walk from the bathroom to the front room four months ago. There was a little fear; maybe walking the dog would be too much for me. The moment I thought about walking, I could tell he was tuned in. Pretty soon, his enthusiasm spread to me.

What a feat to get a collar on a prancing ninety pound dog!

Life Lesson Number One: Be enthusiastic about life.

We piled into the car. Houdini's excitement was so great I imagined I could hear him just like a kid saying, "When we gonna get there? When we gonna get there?" A smile began to spread across my face. The next thing I know Houdini is falling into the dashboard of the car. Whoops! I forgot to tell him riding with Sharron was different than riding with Steve.

He's okay; he's a smart learner. He promptly planted his butt on the seat, and poked his nose out the window. He smelled the air; taking deep breaths, and noticing all the sights. He was totally engaged in the moment. His body shivered with excitement, as we arrived.

He lunged out of the car. "Let's go. I have places to go and things to do." His attitude was contagious. I couldn't wait to see what he was going to do. As we headed down the path, he tuned in and sniffed the air, listening for sounds of the animals and birds, and just enjoying the sun.

Life Lesson Number Two: Live in the moment. Be engaged with what you're doing.

He was on alert as he watched with sharp eyes. As we walked alongside the water, Houdini suddenly seized the moment and lunged into the water while tromping on a dead fish. Boy was he fast! He snatched the fish out of the water, and shook it all over the place. "I am master!" Yes, he was master, and I was now fish - wet and doomed to smell his fish breath on the ride home.

Time passed quickly! I didn't even think about how hard walking usually was for me. Finally, I told Houdini that I needed time out. We found a bench. I gave him a lesson in being patient and still. That lasted until he suddenly spied quacking ducks.

Houdini's nose popped up, his body on point. He was still as a rock and was ready for attack. "Come on Houdini," I said, "that's for another day. "As we started back, Houdini made the most of every opportunity as it presented itself - peeing on every rock, bush, and plant along the way, even when the pee ran out. I laughed

Life Lesson Number Three: Seize the moment.

I realized I had set my goals too high. We had gone too far for me to walk. Houdini, being the good friend he is, pulled me up the last hill.

Life Lesson Number Four: If you set your goals high, be prepared to accept help.

I told Houdini we had to go home. He made a groan.

Now back in the living room, his ninety pounds are crammed on my lap. He is an opportunist who takes a hug anytime it is offered. I began to fall asleep and so did he. My last thought was, "I'd better bring in my grandson's jeans off the back porch or Houdini will eat them."

Life Lesson Number Five: Ask for a hug when you need it.

> Everything we do is an act of poetry or a painting if we do it with mindfulness.
>
> ~*Thich Nhat Hanh*

Stress as an Addiction

Positive stress is natural and as humans we experience stress as early as in the mother's womb. Learning to cope with stress as a function of normal development and motivation which helps us develops skills to adapt to life.

Even though there is a positive role for stress, our bodies can become used to being negatively stressed that we do not even notice it. Chronic stress piles up, and when it reaches a critical mass, it is difficult to recover from it. Stress that took place years ago can still affect you in the present.

The benefits of stress diminish when they become severe enough to overwhelm a person. This overwhelm is considered toxic stress, often resulting in intense unpleasant experiences. Toxic stress can disrupt brain development, compromise immune functioning, and affect the nervous system.

High levels of stress hormones are produced as long as a person is stressed. These hormones can suppress learning and memory. A stressed response system can lead to many health problems such as depression, heart disease, panic attacks, and other chronic illnesses.

Stress accompanied by an addictive component can be difficult to disconnect from. The stress addiction cycles as follows:

- Initial stress.
- "I wish life wasn't like this."

- ♥ Regret and guilt.
- ♥ "I'll do better."
- ♥ Disgrace and despair.
- ♥ Intention to remove stressors.
- ♥ Fears of failure and rejection.
- ♥ Disappointed expectations and anger.
- ♥ Poor functioning and performance.
- ♥ Increased stress.

Like any addiction, stress itself can function as a high. The stress high can feed the ego with self-pride. Self-pride manifests as the ego wanting you to think that you're better than the rest, or the most beautiful, or the most sensitive, etc.

Positive or negative, the ego likes extremes and always wants to stand out and be special. It always wants others to have a strong opinion of you – good or bad. On the opposite end, the ego may also want to prove that you're the most misunderstood, the most miserable, the cruelest, the most hurt, or the most anything. It can create a get-even mentality.

A physical component of being addicted to stress is in the production of adrenalin. The adrenalin rush can prompt a feeling of being alive, and as with addiction to anything, the seeker seeks it over and over again. Ask yourself if you are addicted to stress. Addiction to stress can cause you to emotionally overreact, seek constant stimuli for the fight or fight rush, or defend your ego regardless of the negativity it brings to your relationships.

Soul Exercise 4: Simple Meditation

Always do meditation in a relaxing, private place. You may tape record this meditation and play it back.

- First, before you even sit down, set your intention. Remember your goal in meditating. Recall that, like all spiritual practices, meditation is an action for you. Begin by sitting comfortably, with your spine upright. You may use a chair, a bench, or a cushion. Starting at the top of your head, scan down throughout your body.

- Noticing tension in your muscles and relax them. Repeat the relaxation scan two or three times at your own pace.

- Next, place your attention on your breathing. Do not change the breathing, just bring awareness to it and stay with it in a relaxed manner. If you find your attention wandering, gently bring it back to the breath, over and over and over again. If you have great struggle staying with the breath, try counting breaths for a while.

- Mentally count the breath from 1 to 10, and then start over at one. Keep your primary attention on the sensations of the breath. If you lose count start over at one. Eventually you can drop the counting and just be with the breath.

- Gradually your mind will settle down, your consciousness will start to emerge. Settle into the quiet and stillness; notice the divineness of your body. Your heart and body will relax and your soul will expand.

- Finally, count to five and bring your awareness back to the room.

Choose Your Words Wisely

Stress is sometimes created through the words we speak, because words carry either positive or negative energy. There is wisdom in consciously choosing your words. There's probably not anyone who hasn't, at some time, felt self-loathing for the words they have spoken.

Miguel Ruiz's book, *The Four Agreements, a Practical Guide to Personal Freedom,* talks about being impeccable with your word. Arguing or gossiping about someone sends out negative energy often causing stress. Saying something kind or generous sends out positive energy promoting peace. Being mindful of your word energy can reduce your stress dramatically. Ruiz notes that being impeccable with your word means you speak with integrity and truth with love. Here are my affirmations:

- ♥ I intend to be impeccable with my words by focusing on saying what I mean.
- ♥ I aim to speak with integrity.
- ♥ I plan to avoid gossip.
- ♥ I set my intentions to use the power of my words in the direction of truth and love.

Recently, I purchased Ruiz's next book, *The Fifth Agreement, a Practical Guide to Self Mastery.* I was surprised when I saw that I missed a valuable part of being impeccable with my word. Ruiz notes being impeccable with your word especially means never using the power of word against yourself. He comments when you're impeccable with your word, you never betray yourself. I squirmed when I read that sentence.

Ruiz tells us it is the ultimate self-betrayal and disloyalty to use the power of word against ourselves. Often when we make a mistake, we call ourselves names. Common negative self talk is: "I'm fat." "I'm stupid." "I can't do that." "No one will like me." As we speak these words to ourselves, we script negativity on our subconscious mind. The subconscious then acts the scripted words out in our physical reality.

It's hard enough to live in the world today with people who are willing to use harmful words against us. Negative self words are more powerful than what other people say about us, because we speak them more frequently. When we use harmful words against ourselves we cause self-stress. When we practice speaking loving self words we send healing energy.

> Worry weighs a person down and encouraging words cheer a person up.
>
> ~Proverbs 12:25

Soul Exercise 5: The Power of Words

How many times do you complain? Pick one day this week to go without complaining. Carry a piece of paper with you and record when you slip up and complain. After twenty-four hours, count how many times you slipped. Was there a pattern to your complaining? If so, what limiting belief do you need to release to step out of complaining? What behavior do you need to change? Create a positive affirmation opposite of the limiting belief or behavior. Use self-hypnosis daily with the new positive affirmation.

The Power of Silence

Learning to use positive words is important, but learning when to stay quiet also can be essential. Recently, I was attracted to the book, *When to Speak Up and When to Shut Up*, by Dr. Michael D. Sedler who says that you will walk in peace, if you learn to stay silent in the face of anger. He further states the more you try to defend yourself in the face of someone else's anger, the more you enter into conflict with that person. What a hard lesson to learn!

I had to laugh, because *When to Speak Up and When to Shut Up* immediately took me back to memories of my father. My father was a master of knowing when to shut up. He kept six kids in line when we got angry or just plain ornery, by looking at us over the top of his glasses with absolute silence. He knew how to have peace in the midst of mayhem. Dad knew that silence was his perfect weapon against words. He also chose his words carefully so that he did not enter into anger himself.

As each of us grew up, we knew Dad really listened to what we said. He was fully and totally present, not wandering away in his own thoughts. He knew the wisdom of not making assumptions, overreacting, or jumping to conclusions. Dad was never one to let his mind react by negatively assuming something was wrong, or someone was in trouble. He listened to all our complaints, and then he asked us for solutions to the problem we presented. He was willing to hear our ideas, even when he was aggravated with us.

My dad has since passed away, but his example has continued to make a profound impact on my interactions with my art, with my clients, and with my life. When a client walks in the door, I clear my mind so I can listen fully to what the person has to say. Often, it's more productive to listen carefully to what people are silent about. When people are involved in their personal conflict, I share with them Dad's technique of remaining silent at the appropriate time. Dad lives in my heart in every action I take. I remember the power of silence he taught us.

Rhyming Time

~Sharron Magyar

You are so selfish, you think only of you
Hold up that armor with angry words.
Rapping of anger and jive, just trying to stay alive,
All the while you are dead to what's really in your head.
Verse and rhyme, just trying to keep the time,
Stealing every-one else's energy,
Never stopping to think about,
The garbage coming out of your mouth.
Verse, rhyme and time, not just talk about violence,
But violent thoughts in your head.
Only words, in the end could be your death.

Stress and Worry Are Best Buddies

We worry. At times, worry can be helpful for us, if it initiates a response to a problem in a positive way. However, when your life becomes chronically stuck in worry, it can be problematic. Chronic worry is the habit of exaggerating the possibility of danger, out of proportion to its likelihood. Stop and think of how many times you have worried about something that never came to pass. Worry causes your body to respond in a constant state of ready alert, consuming a great deal of your energy.

Thought forms remain inactive in the energy field until they are activated by energetic thought. Most thoughts go in and out of the energy field, however, worry thought forms are different. They pile up, jamming the energy field. A vicious cycle is perpetuated by the attraction of similar worry energy, - from the self as well as others. Thoughts and feelings increase, eventually developing into chronic worry. Chronic worry then mutates into physical illness in the body causing high blood pressure, heart disease, and diabetes as well as other illnesses.

I don't know about you, but I don't have energy to waste these days. To dissolve worry thought forms, take time to express and release emotion connected to the thought form. You may choose connect with the subconscious with hypnosis, meditation, breathwork, or massage.

> Can all your worries add a single moment to your life? And why worry about your clothing? Look at the lilies in the field and how they grow. They don't work or make their clothing, yet Solomon in all of his glory was not dressed as beautiful as they are.
>
> ~Matthew 6:27-29

Soul Exercise 6: Creative Visualization

Always do meditation in a relaxing, private place. You may tape record this meditation and play it back.

Make a list of what you would eliminate from your life if you had only one month to live. Then make a list of how to create happiness in your life, include the things you love to do. For one month, act on your lists and notice your internal and external changes.

- ♥ Visualize (in your mind's eye) what you want to achieve. Spend time and energy focusing on it. Your subconscious mind will perceive it as achievable, because it does not evaluate. . . . It does not question, "Can I, or can I not, do it?" Your subconscious simply accepts the visualization and brings the plan into action.

- ♥ Meditate, (you can use body scan meditation) step into your senses. How would it feel to have what you desire? What can you hear people saying? Feel it in your body! See it as real in your mind, as if you were there.

Listening To Your Instincts

In my work I often hear complaints such as, "I can't sleep." "I don't have energy." "I am in continual pain." "My family is driving me nuts." "I don't have any time for myself," and so forth. What is really happening for the person is they are experiencing power loss. Interestingly enough power loss can be outside of conscious awareness.

Power loss can manifest itself in many different ways. One symptom of power loss is a severe reduction in energy, with a sense of inertia and powerlessness. Other symptoms show themselves as:

- ♥ Low self-esteem.
- ♥ Self-depreciation.
- ♥ Low-grade illness.
- ♥ Recurrent mishaps.
- ♥ Continual bad luck.

- 💚 Feeling disconnected from loved ones.
- 💚 Feeling out of control.
- 💚 Having panic attacks.

Power loss can drive a person to be a workaholic, getting less done but spending more time trying. It can also be experienced as an inability to maintain boundaries.

We all cooperate with our own power loss to some degree, by failing to listen to our instincts and to our bodies. To make matters worse, society pushes us to give away our power every day. It persuades us to give up our authenticity - instead of being true to ourselves.

Advertisements promote that we must buy "something" in order to be special. Movies and television set unrealistic standards for our daily lives as well as our bodies. Anorexia is encouraged, artificial breasts and lips will bring you happiness, never mind the cost and health risk.

How do you prevent personal power loss? First, use your freewill, and do not allow yourself to be manipulated or coerced against your better judgment. Learn to say "no" and draw the line against those people and actions which cause you to lose power. In circumstances when people try to bend your will to theirs, it's okay to be selfish and attend to your needs first. Remove yourself from those situations. You cannot be good to others, if you cannot be good to yourself first.

Personal power can also be lost by being out of integrity. If your actions are not living up to your words, you are invalidating your own code of honor. For example, if you continually tell people you will say or do something, and you fail to follow up on your words, you lose personal power.

If other people's actions do not line up with their words, it may be time to remove or redefine yourself in relationship to them.

Connect to sources of personal power such as music, books, sports, pets, friends, and art. They open you to blessings and empowerment. You are the only person who can make time for them.

Soul Exercises # 7: Reinvent Your Day

Always do meditation in a relaxing, private place. You may tape record this meditation and play it back.

Have you ever had a night when you lay your head down to sleep, and worry thoughts roll around in your head? You worry about what you said and did that day. You worry about what tomorrow will bring. You continuously worry about your children, your parents, or your performance at work or school. Here's the question:

Did any of the worry bring you comfort or resolution? The answer would probably be "no." Worry before sleeping expends energy during sleep. You can learn to save your energy and disconnect from worry by using the following technique:

At night when you lie down to sleep, go through the events of the day. If you come to a thought or an action that you regret or wish you had done differently, visualize that same event with a positive outcome, and then forget about it. Let the event go and fall asleep with your new visualization. You will be scripting your subconscious mind with a blueprint for dealing with a similar issue in the future, and you will fall asleep with a clearer energy field. The goal is to attract positive energy in your life through pre-sleep visualization. This also prevents you from losing energy through worry. Spending your energy worrying about a problem attracts that problem to you. Spend the same energy on the solution to the problem, and your life will be changed powerfully.

> No one is in control of your happiness but you; therefore, you have the power to change anything about yourself or your life that you want to change.
>
> ~Barbara de Angelis

5
The Inner Child

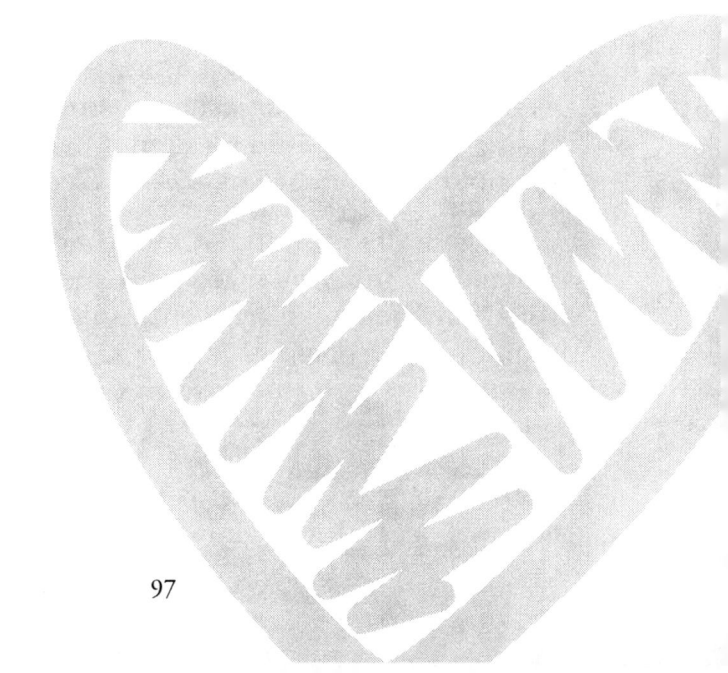

Many people have within themselves a healthy inner child who views life with happiness and creativity, and carries these healthy characteristics into adult life to provide relief from stressful adult conflicts. Other people carry an inner child who has been wounded, rendering it difficult to cope with normal adult challenges. A wound can be caused by sexual abuse, physical abuse, loss of a loved one, traumatic surgery, natural disaster, or loss of a pet, to name a few.

The wound can be inflicted from a seemingly insignificant event, yet it negatively impacts the child due to the way the *child interprets the event*. Additionally, a child can be wounded by witnessing a traumatic event. Wounding forms an imprint in a child's energy field, chakras, and body.

I have spent a lifetime trying to understand the energetic effect trauma has on a child. A traumatized child can energetically leave the body, to protect themselves from pain. If this occurs, energy can become fractured and open to dark attachments. For an in-depth study focusing on dark energy attachments that exert control over a child's thoughts and behaviors, refer to *Remarkable Healings* by Shakuntala Modi, M.D.

Another energetic effect from childhood trauma is the diversion of energy from normal growth and learning. Diverted energy encapsulates trauma in the body, often causing partial or full blocks in a child's memory. "Time" does not move forward in these walled off experiences.

Energetically, a traumatized child also has the ability to maintain individualized and distinct personalities for protection. Prolonged or severe trauma can cause the creation of multiple personalities. It takes a professional specializing in multiple personality disorder to reintegrate developed personalities.

Energy is energy. What is important is that diversion of energy is needed to maintain survival of a wound. If pain is great enough the "fight or flight state" is activated. Once activated, it can become stuck in its activation and usurp a tremendous amount of the child's energy. A stuck "fight or flight state" interferes with learning, and often causes continual physical discomfort such as stomach aches and headaches for the child.

The adult, who is carrying a wounded inner child with soul loss, often rejects work challenges, avoids employment, and rebels against authority. Wounds inflicted in childhood remain throughout adulthood until the trauma is released in some way.

Energetically, a wounded child can have a hole in their soul; which can cause feelings of being alone and lost. A child may also have energetic cords extending from the abuser to the child, which allow the abuser to steal the child's soul energy and hold it captive.

When a wound is incurred, the inner child's emotions and beliefs (such as guilt, shame, fear and grief) become locked in time. As the child becomes an adult, these emotions play out as self-criticism, co-dependency and self-destructive behavior. Many of us know someone who functions as a child in an adult body.

As important as it is to consider what is happening energetically to a child when they experience trauma, we must also realize that globally, stress is at an all-time high for children. Hunger issues, concerns about physical safety, and monetary problems are ever increasing in today's society. These issues daily increase childhood stress levels.

Childhood Stress

I volunteered to help with a school project and I wondered what I had gotten myself into. I walked in the door, and there were kids all over the place. I have never before seen so many kids excited to be at school before, especially on a Saturday. This school project was aimed at addressing stress factors which limit, effect, and frustrate kids.

According to the *Cambridge Dictionary*, stress is defined as "great worry caused by a difficult situation or something which causes this condition." Stressors develop for children through many avenues, but again remember, the perception a child has of an event makes the event a stressor. (Hale, 1998)

Many kids today have a unique pattern of stressors but it is not always easy to see what they are. Throughout history, predators have physically, emotionally, and sexually abused children. It is invaluable when a child is able to openly talk about abuse, and when there is a rapid response by those in authority. However, many children never speak of their abuse. Physical or sexual abuse can cause extreme stress in young children, which then is reflected in emotions such as despair, frustration, anger, and powerlessness. (Hale, 1998)

Life's stressors impact a child's ability to process information and to learn. It has been documented that intelligence and performance problems may be caused by an accumulation of chronic stress factors. *The Effects of Childhood Stress on Health Across The Lifespan* published by the U.S. Department of Health and Human Services notes; "The ability to manage stress is controlled by brain circuits that circulate throughout the body."

Prolonged exposure to stress hormones can impact the brain and impair functioning in a variety of ways. Early childhood stress can result in:

- Disruption of the neural pathways of the brain.
- Suppression of the body's immune system.
- Damage to the hippocampus, the area of the brain responsible for learning & memory.
- Development of a smaller brain.

According to the ACE study, collaboration between the Centers for Disease Control and Prevention and Kaiser Permanente's Health Appraisal Clinic in San Diego, stress has a debilitating effect on cognition. Stress initiates changes in cortisol levels and the activity of neurons which suppress memory, attention span, and self-regulation.

Academic pressure put on children through demands for educational performance can stress a child. (Helms 1996) Pressure to pass their ACT for admission into college, as well as school work itself can be a stressor. Children can fear both success and failure in the school setting.

Many families today experience economic hardship. These stressors take the form of: lack of money, lack of cleanliness and comfort, and an unsafe home environment. (Moos, 2004) Additionally, social factors can be stressful for a child as parents can have too little or too much parental interest in their child.

Violence is on the rise domestically, in the school, and in the community, contributing to childhood stress. Dustin Racioppi of the Asbury Park (N.J.) Press on April 11, 2013 notes: according to the defense fund in 2010, 15,576 children and teenagers were injured by firearms — three times more than the number of U.S. soldiers injured in the war in Afghanistan.

The New England Journal of Medicine also states: "Nationally, guns still kill twice as many children and young people than cancer, five times as many than heart disease, and 15 times more than infection." Many children experience stress walking out of their houses to play because of safety issues. If that isn't enough, violence in the media and video games is at all time high level.

Often, stress for a child is not contained in childhood, but is carried long into adulthood. No matter how old a child becomes, any event that is similar to his/her original triggering event, can cause the child to regress physically and/or emotionally to the first stressor. Detailed sensory and emotional perceptions of the original stressor are typical.

When stress levels become extreme, the subconscious protects the child from stress overload. Stressful events remain embedded and carried in the inner child's subconscious until the energy is somehow released. What is unexpressed in the subconscious often appears in the body as physical and mental illness as well as pain.

Programs such as the one I volunteered for are important to help children recognize and cope with stress. We must keep in mind the energetic repercussions of stress on a child and identify and eliminate it.

Soul Exercise 8: Healing Fears

If you suspect your child is stressed, ask him or her to draw a picture of what they are worried about. Once they have that picture drawn, ask them to draw a picture of the worry "all better." Ask them how do they see it all better? When do they feel it in their body? When is it all better?

Help your child use all of his/her senses when experiencing it better. What do they hear people saying when it is all better? Then have him/her draw a picture of how they made it all better. When your child is finished he/she will have two pictures; one of the worry, the other of the worry healed.

Because the subconscious does not distinguish if something is real or unreal, this task will often dissolve stress and worry for the child.

My Inner Child

Inner child wounds can be in your conscious awareness or out of your conscious awareness. Often, things happen to us that we don't remember while growing up; nor do we realize the negative impact these events carry into our adult lives. During a personal hypnosis session, I had the following memory:

I saw myself at ten years old; I was standing at the blackboard trying to work a math problem. I had a yucky feeling in the pit of my stomach because I didn't have a clue how to work the problem. I could tell the teacher was frustrated. I was frozen in time, as I stood silently with the chalk in my hand. The teacher tromped over to where I stood and swatted me on the butt. Shame filled my face as I returned to my seat. All I wanted to do was run out of the room, but I knew my mom would be mad at me if I did.

I had completely forgotten that experience. At some level it stayed with me, and in the hypnosis session, my face again filled with shame. When I came out of hypnosis, I realized the importance of that experience.

Growing up we moved a lot and I was always the new student in school. It made learning math hard for me because every time I would start at a new school, the math would be totally different than at the old school. I was a kid; I didn't realize there were gaps in my education in math. Catching up to the new math level was always difficult for me, but I tried as hard as I could.

Until the day of my hypnosis session, I believed, "I am no good at math", and I was ashamed of it. That belief almost kept me out of college. I avoided every math course I had to take until my very last semester. Ironically, and maybe because I had unlocked my childhood experience about math, I did complete all my math courses with straight A's.

My College Fairy

I graduated from Lincoln Land Community College with honors and awards from the Language Arts Department. I was happy and proud of that part of my life because it was one area of which I had control. The rest of my life was spent with the drama Tammy was creating through her addiction. I then decided to continue my education at University of Illinois at Springfield.

Two semesters was all it took for me to figure out that UIS didn't offer the specific education I was looking for, so I started investigating other universities. I kept coming back to the idea of applying at Washington University in St.

Louis. It seemed like the right fit educationally, but there were many obstacles. One was the high expense of two years of college at WU. With my husband just a few years away from retirement, I felt it would be a huge sacrifice for him to support me.

Along with that, the two hundred mile daily roundtrip would be challenging, as I still needed to work a job at home to pay for my education.

One moment I was going to apply, and the next moment I'd say, "Forget it". My husband Steve kept encouraging me saying, "You can do it. You need to do it or you won't be happy with yourself." I finally mustered up the courage to make an appointment with the Dean of the Art Department to apply for admission at Washington University.

I was scared to death. Would my high GPA be enough to get me in? This was primarily a university for kids recently graduating from high school. I could be a token older student in the midst of ten thousand younger students. Would they accept me?

My application required me to bring samples of my paintings for the interview. I picked through the paintings that best represented the different stages of my artwork. At the very last minute, I grabbed a fairy painting. It seemed to want to come with me, so I plucked it off the wall and off we went.

The hour and a half drive from home gave me plenty of time to get in touch with my nervousness. Every negative thought I could think of was rolling around in my head. "What if I can't get in because of my age?" "What if I have to do a lot of math?" "What if they think my artwork is crap?" I certainly hoped to have enough courage to walk through the door after I drove all the way down there. "Just get me there soon before I chicken out," I prayed. That was the longest drive of my life.

When I walked in the door of the Art Department my hands were shaking. I was hoping they didn't notice. As I sat waiting, I wondered, "Maybe I should just leave now."

I stayed.

My turn came to be interviewed. The Dean explained that if I was accepted into the program, I would be interacting with a student population between the ages of eighteen to twenty one. I told him I understood, and didn't see my age as being a handicap. With that out of the way, we progressed to my artwork. I was obviously nervous, but hoped he didn't notice me fidgeting in my chair.

As the Dean looked over all my paintings, I was unsure what he thought of my work. When his eyes landed on the fairy painting, he asked me to tell him about it. My stomach did a flip-flop, and I was silently kicking myself for bringing that stupid painting, (even though I loved it). I took a deep breath. "Should I tell him the truth?" In my mind I thought, "He won't believe it." I'm not a good liar," So I dove in.

Following is the story I shared with him: The art assignment had been to paint a memory from childhood. My mind went back to schooldays when we used to live in the country. Our house had a long lane to walk down in order to catch the school bus. The lane had a fence row running parallel to it.

One day, I was moseying along the lane when all of a sudden I looked up and saw a fairy on the fencepost. It was about twelve inches tall, transparent and light in energy. She was dancing beautifully, just like a ballerina. As I walked to the next fencepost, the fairy appeared on it, and on the next, and then on the next, until the last fencepost. The fairy then quickly disappeared.

Now, even as a child, I knew no one would believe me if I told them what I had seen. I didn't want to be made fun of, so I never told anyone about the fairy until the day I painted her.

As an adult looking back, I've always wondered if I really did see a fairy or if it was my active imagination. I decided it really didn't matter - what did matter was the enchantment that seeing the fairy gave me. I was striving to capture the magic and beauty of the dancing fairy in my painting. The fairy experience opened me to the possibility of unexplainable magic in the world.

The Dean listened to my story carefully. With no idea what he was thinking, I figured I'd blown my chances of getting into this prestigious university. He scrutinized the painting and looked back at me while I was still holding my breath. Then, he said, "You're in." Do this, this and this, "You'll be starting in the fall."

I was laughing all the way home. I felt like singing. I was ecstatic. I was going to Washington University. I was nuts!

Tammy's Inner Child

Frustration had a hold on me with everything we were going through with Tammy. Steve and I were desperate for help. We had to know what had happened to Tammy as a child. We entered family therapy hoping they could help unravel things for us. From the moment we started therapy as a family, none of us liked our therapist, but we committed to give it a try.

Steve, Tammy and I didn't know what therapy was supposed to be like, having nothing to measure or compare our experience. It seemed like such a waste of money and time to be silently sitting in the office while the therapist stared at us. He had nothing to volunteer, no support, no insight and no empathy. As a matter of fact, he rarely talked to us.

What the heck! I was getting madder by the minute at the whole counseling routine. He would ask us, "How do you feel about that?" How did he think I felt? I was angry as hell that I was sitting in a therapy office throwing away my money.

I've often wondered if many people had the same experience with therapy as we did. I wasn't looking for magic; I was looking for help with my child and my family. I knew Steve and I were at wit's end. We were having a difficult time understanding what we were paying for. We continued with therapy hoping for a change for the better at some point. Whatever the answers were, the timing was not right to discover what had happened to Tammy's inner child.

A Picture is Worth a Million Words

~Sharron Magyar

Tammy has a huge smile on her face,

Intelligence laughing in her eyes.

Catching her dad's fish he put in the pond that day;

Skating upon the pond,

Hating to stop for a drink.

Riding her pony and playing games or pretend.

Reading <u>Cat in the Hat</u> over and over again,

Memorizing every word,

Dressing up in old clothes, cooking with mom,

Learning tricks of the trade,

Smearing cookies all over her face; stumbling on her toes.

God forgot to give her balance and grace.

Picking all the neighbors' flowers for my vase;

And the picture changes at about ten.

The smile gone, disappeared, in its place a sober expression.

Nightmares begin to set in, weariness,

Tears in a frustrated place.

Where did my laughing girl go, and who took her place?

It is so silent, so quiet at first, I don't notice at all,

And then I realize one day, something is out of place.

I search and search, what could it be?

For me just an intuition, a feeling,

Gnawing at my subconscious mind,

Not quite in the open, yet won't go away.

What happened to my girl of yesterday?

Inherited Soul Loss

A child can be born into a tragic family life situation with stress impacting the child at birth. When a child needs healing, the issue to be addressed may be with the child, or may originate with one or both of the parents.

I am the oldest child in my family. A year after I came into the world, my sister, Dixie Marie, was born. At one month old, she unexpectedly died. Betty was born a year after Dixie Marie's death. I remember my mom saying Betty cried nonstop when she was a baby.

As an adult, I realize Betty was born, while my parents were grieving the loss of their second child. Betty, even as an infant, felt the unresolved grief my parents were experiencing. To make matters worse she had the task of building her personality, while my parent's grieved. What a testament to her resiliency as a baby.

Betty's Comment: *All of my growing up days, I was puzzled why I always felt like I didn't belong to my family. It wasn't until the age of fifty that events in my life brought to light the issues related to my birth and bonding with both parents. The pieces for me finally fell into place, and at long last I understood the source of my feelings of not being accepted.*

Toxic Parents

Not only can an infant have wounded parents, sometimes a child has toxic parents. Toxic parents often cannot provide physical, mental /or emotional support, and they have difficulty giving their child a safe environment. An emotionally bankrupt parent frequently seeks ways to meet their own needs, leading them to behave inappropriately with an infant or child. (Example: The parent can expect the child to be the caretaker.)

A toxic parent may appear to be a loving parent to society, yet at home they can transfer abuse and neglect to their offspring. Problems may be influenced by traumas suffered in the family's prior generations, yet those presently affected now, have no awareness of the original wounding event.

A theoretical basis for this concept is called the ancestor syndrome in psychology. In the book *The Ancestor Syndrome*, Anne Ancelin Schutzenberger gives details and provides scientific examples with her distinctive genealogical approach. She shows how generations are linked together.

The events and traumas that our ancestors lived through impact our own lifetime, and are therefore out of our conscious awareness. Healing the inner child can positively affect the child's parents through generational healing.

Pages of Time

~Sharron Magyar

A thought is caught between the pages of time
There one moment, vanishing the next.
A child's cry echoes upon the pages of time, alone,
Unheard, and disappearing in the darkness of night.
Lost, aborted to the moment in time, falling on deaf ears.
Never mind, for God did hear.
Like raindrops falling upon the water,
Upon the pages of time are written their waves,
Silently sending out messages,
Forever changing the Universe.

Tribal Connections

One thing that is constant across all cultures is the development of a child's personal identity with their tribe. A child's tribe includes parents of origin, surrogate parents, aunts, uncles, cousins and neighbors. If members of a child's tribe are healthy and well positioned, a child will develop a strong identity.

If a child's tribe is unhealthy, either physically or mentally, it can negatively influence the child. The child may develop personality traits based on fear and weakness, rather than strength and affirmative beliefs necessary to good health. Fear and weakness sets the foundation for childhood energetic soul loss, which results in the child not having enough energy to appropriately move through each developmental stage. Soul loss also prevents a child from becoming a healthy functioning adult.

When the ethical code of behavior is broken from generation to generation, it produces children who develop maladaptive ways of coping with the world. In many generations, sexual and physical abuse is passed down within the tribe, causing soul loss in children. As soul loss is passed through generations, it has a larger impact on the current generation, than the previous generation. Healing just one person in a genetic line can have a positive impact for generations to come.

Repercussions of maladaptive coping become more apparent as children become adults. Children who come from a wounded tribe often become adults who avoid intimate relationships and friendships, mistrust everyone, and are locked into negativity and isolation.

I would offer that soul loss has led to moral and emotional numbness as well as increased drug use. Lack of honor, loyalty, or spiritual foundation, can cause society to be broken from within contributing to collective soul loss.

The sacredness of life has long been celebrated in many cultures, yet in our society, we have moved away from this age old custom. Carl Jung says that for a thousand years, rights of initiation have taught regeneration of the spirit. Could it be that the absence of important "rites of passage" can contribute to soul loss in some individuals and groups?

"Rites of passage" mark the passage from one phase of

your life to another, or can be personal events marking all sorts of occasions. Examples are birth of a child, the transition from child to adult, and marriage.

To make a case for "rites of passage," one of the most daunting experiences my husband faced as a soldier occurred in his home town. Many Viet Nam veterans were spat upon by the public. The Viet Nam War was unpopular. Society fell short in their appreciation of the men who in good faith fought for our country. As a returning Viet Nam soldier, Steve's community did not welcome him home.

As a group, veterans comprise one of the most heartbreaking examples of soul loss today. First they experience the trauma of combat, and then encounter rejection by society. Soldiers returning from war, long to reconnect to the people of the country they left behind to protect.

It took forty years for someone to shake my husband's hand and tell him, "Welcome home, brother." What a beautiful day of healing for my husband's soul.

As a society, I believe we have learned from our mistreatment of Viet Nam veterans and we are determined to do better, by providing opportunities for veterans to reconnect positively with society. Communities are uniting, holding parades, awarding social acknowledgement, as well as performing other "rites of passage" for returning veterans.

Group traumas are another way tribal connections are challenged. In the twenty-first century, we have encountered 9-11, the earthquake in Japan, and floods of New Orleans, and the Boston Marathon bombings - all examples of events that can lead to collective soul loss.

You can rebuild the neighborhood, but you must address soul loss for the group to heal. The group can both become stronger and find healing from the experience by accepting opportunities initiated by the catastrophe, or they may stay "frozen in time" by the event. Soul loss is indicated when people say, "That was the day that changed my life. I was never the same after that."

Our task as individuals is to develop the process of individuation, which means breaking free from what does not serve us well, and adopt beliefs that support our personal development. Personal tribal connections either support or stunt the individuation process.

As a society, we can support positive changes by taking action. Reinforcing community through love and celebration can provide the nurturing environment to support flourishing individuals. Joining in partnership to share that which honors self and nature fosters positive tribal connections.

Creating "rites of passage" provides numerous healing opportunities, allowing people to both personally and collectively heal.

Trauma Imprints

Imprints are a natural part of childhood development and shape the instinctual aspect of behavior. One of the most easily recognizable imprints is a child's bond with his parents. Parental imprints are carried with a person through their entire life, and they generally bring love and joy to the child. Positive imprinting leads to useful beliefs.

Imprinting is a term used to describe any kind of learning that occurs at a particular age combined with a specific life stage, which is rapid and independent of the consequences of behavior. Imprints are relatively resistant to forgetting or extinction.

A person can be traumatically imprinted given the right developmental stage, combined with a painful event. To make matters worse, subsequent traumatic imprinting reinforces original painful imprinting. Injurious imprinting leads to limiting beliefs and feelings such as frustration, failure, loneliness, worthlessness, and a sense of being stuck in life. Even though imprints are irreversible, they can be neutralized.

All imprints have a psychological, neurological and physical basis. Imprinted learning occurs in the subconscious and can drive your behavior, "out of your conscious awareness."

If a child was sexually abused at an early age, the imprint on the child's emotion reads, "to be loved means you must be hurt." Every single time the child is looking for love, the child is also looking for someone to hurt them.

The belief is not just psychological; it's neurological as well, because "love hurts" has been imprinted on every cell. Developmental timing is critical to imprinting. An example of timing is a negative sexual imprint at puberty can lead to sexual perversion, fetishism, etc.

The primary characteristic of a negative imprint is that *freewill has been taken out of the equation*. If a person does not have free will in a particular area of their life, it is possible early negative imprinting exists. An imprinted person's response is consistent regardless of the self-damage that each response creates.

A child with a negative imprint can grow up to be an adult who repeatedly seeks out dysfunctional, painful relationships. The above example is just one imprint; there are numerous negative emotional imprints a person can hold, yet it only takes one to have a devastating effect on the individual.

Negative imprints lead to maladaptive beliefs such as *I am defective, I am a failure, I am un-loveable, and I can't trust anyone.*

Negative emotional imprinting is a result of soul wounds at a deep level. A negative imprint can be painlessly addressed through the mind/body connection. Neurolinguistic Programming techniques combine humming, sound, and imagery, neutralizing an imprint.

Sound therapy also works well, because it utilizes energetic sound frequencies to deconstruct the imprinting, and then harmonizes the mind-body rhythms. Specific sounds ultimately realign energy to help heal the body.

The biggest obstacle in removing imprints is recognizing that the imprint exists in the first place. Few practitioners have the experience and finesse to neutralize emotional imprints. Ask questions, look at credentials and do your research before choosing to work with a professional.

Trauma incurred during the imprinting stages can leave long lasting effects which reduce flexibility and shut out possibilities that would otherwise be open.

The next example is of Raymond's inner child. This will help you understand how his childhood imprint of losing his mother at age five created lifelong mistrust and suspicion. His imprint at an early age was that he could not trust those he loved to be there for him, and he could not trust life to provide safety and security.

Raymond's Inner Child

Sometimes ignorance can be beneficial. Both Raymond and I had no idea we were about to begin an incredible journey to heal his inner child. It started with the two of us sitting on a blanket, enjoying the sun in the park. We could feel a soft breeze on our faces as we heard the birds singing. The sky was a beautiful blue with white fluffy clouds here and there.

I asked Raymond if he could allow himself to become peaceful and listen to my voice. When I saw he was fully relaxed, I asked him to go back in time to the best place to begin his life story. His mind took him back, and he saw himself standing in the front yard of his childhood home. He focused his awareness on that day, and started to recount it.

Raymond recalled that he had been pouting and whining at his mom for a sandwich. There was no bread in the house. His Mom was exasperated with him. Finally, she and his aunt got in the car to go to the grocery store to buy bread. Raymond was standing in the front yard watching them while they left.

He saw the car pull out of the driveway and start across the railroad tracks nearby. He heard a loud screeching noise. The car was crushed by the train in front of his eyes. He didn't comprehend what had really happened; all he could see was mangled metal and a stopping train. People began running toward the car and Raymond ran, too. He had to see what was happening. He didn't know why everyone was milling around the train.

No one noticed Raymond standing amongst the people. He couldn't find his mother; he didn't know where she had gone. In one small second, the stage had been set for him to lose a part of his soul, and to feel abandonment for the rest of his life.

Frozen In Fear

Raymond's inner child is an example of a child stuck in fear with a soul wound which embedded in his body. Raymond and fear began a lifelong relationship. Until he went inward to look at his pain, every thought and reaction for forty years was to be made with fear in his heart.

The first consideration in a childhood soul wound is the physical effect of the wounding. There is a difference between having a healthy fear of something, such as fire; and having an unhealthy fear, such as continually being afraid of getting physically hurt.

The body quickly reacts to fear by transferring strong hormones to various body systems that power the "flight or fight" response. Repeated patterns of unhealthy fears can cause the body to get stuck in the "fight or flight" response. If a child repeatedly experiences fear, the **brain** can eventually become wired for a higher level of fear.

Fear physically increases hormone secretions; raises blood pressure, and generate extreme stress which depletes the immune system. Distortion of time and depth perception often accompany situations of extreme fear.

The second consideration of childhood soul wounds is the affect fear has in the individual's life in general. Malfunctions of the fear impulse cause the body to feel the side effects of fear, even when there is nothing to fear.

Can you imagine a child sitting in a class trying to learn, when they are in a constant state of fear? To make matters worse, we live in a society which perpetuates fear in the minds of people in school, at work and in politics.

Childhood soul wounds end up being adult soul wounds, if not released. The resulting fear limits the growth of personality. Fearful people often believe they have to control everything to have power. It takes energy to transcend fear consciousness: it is a limiting, governing and unrelenting state of expectancy.

Authentic power, however, is energy accumulated by existing in the moment, rather than in fear.

There are two common fears that regularly prey upon people - the fear of rejection and fear of failure. Courage can stop fear in its tracks, if you're willing to move forward in spite of it. How does a person carrying an inner child that is frozen in fear move beyond it?

First, as an adult, fear must be acknowledged. Accepting emotional responsibility is beneficial in releasing the idea of being a victim. The difficulty is not what we fear. It is that we do not love and trust ourselves and our higher power - when we are afraid.

Soul Exercise 9: Live Fearlessly

Always do meditation in a relaxing, private place. You may tape record this meditation and play it back.

- Put your body into relaxation. Ask yourself if it is ok to accept your feeling of fear? Can you give yourself permission to release your fear? If the answer is yes, call forth your fear. Allow yourself to just be with your feelings and imagery for a moment. Create in your mind a picture that represents what you are afraid of. Accept and observe the feelings that surface. Ask - What does your fear look like? What color represents your fear? Does it have a shape? Does it have texture? What would it feel like if you touched it? Does it have a smell?

- Create imagery to release your fear. Some people, depending on the emotional content, may choose to blow up the fear. Others may simply choose to transform it into something more positive. Make changes to your imagery which intuitively seems right for you.

- Once you have released the fear, check in with your body. How does it feel? (Sometimes it takes the body longer to record the changes, than it takes the mind.) If the fear is still recorded in your body, you may have to release another fear. Again, go back to another time in your life, when you felt the same fear. Repeat the same process using the questions at the beginning of the exercise until you no longer feel fear in your body.

- When you are complete count to five and bring your awareness back to the room.

Fear

~Sharron Magyar

Fear that I may fail, setting emotions on end;
Conflict being my friend, all that I have learned.
Risk with my vulnerability, old habits die hard,
Or not die at all, sneaking up easily.
Will I be strong, or will I be wrong?
I shake with fear, the lure ready by my own mind;
Vulnerability easing from my pores, drawing more fear.
Will I pass the test? Or will I fail,
My mind locking me in this misery?
How do I release fear to be free?

David

David was an angry young boy who grew up to be an angry adult. David had some hard things happen to him when he was young, that no child should have to experience. He wanted to find love and a happy life. Every time he did find happiness and love, his angry inner boy kept coming out to spoil everything by displaying temper tantrums. He would yell and scream at everyone anytime he was frightened, or felt forced to do something he didn't want to do.

The adult David was frustrated, and knew he wanted happiness. He simply didn't know what to do about the little boy within. He heard that meditating was good for eliminating anger, so he decided to start meditating.

In his first attempt at meditating, it was difficult to get the angry little boy to settle down long enough to become calm and relaxed. The adult David was determined. The next day, David found it unproblematic to relax, and by the time his meditation was over, he could feel his angry little boy calming down.

On the third day, meditation was easier, and David saw an eagle in his meditation. He found it strange that the eagle could talk to him. The eagle asked David to follow him down a forest trail. After a while, the eagle stopped at a cave, and hovered. He told David to call to the guardian of the cave, and ask permission to enter.

When he called, a monk named Rhyocho appeared; he coolly appraised David asking, "Are you sure you're ready for what you may see?" David replied, "Yes, I am ready; I want to change my life."

David was afraid to enter the cave alone, and asked if the eagle could come with him. Rhyocho nodded his head and moved away from the door he was guarding to grant David entrance. As he moved into the cave, he was afraid and nervous. Although it was dark, he was determined to see what was there for him.

The cave was cool, dank and dusty, and he sensed no one had been in it in a long time. David weaved his way into the center of the cave where he discovered a fire. Assuming he was to sit by the fire, he settled onto the ground by a stone. The eagle perched above him on the rock ledge.

As David stared into the fire, he began to see visions flickering on the cave wall - pictures of all of people who had hurt him as a child. They faded in, they faded out. There were many people who had hurt him. He felt like he'd been stabbed in the heart, with anguish as he had never before experienced. David cried and cried at some of the pictures. He had forgotten how badly he was hurt. There were some wounds that he didn't even know were there. His sadness was great. He cried until there were no more tears. Eventually, he fell into a deep sleep.

David awakened with no idea of how much time had passed, yet knew his time was up in the cave. He was still thinking about some of the things he'd seen. Somehow, by recognizing all the difficult events, a burden had been taken off his shoulders. He and his eagle exited the cave. The eagle told him he would meet him in the meadow at the next meditation.

David needed time to process everything he'd seen in the cave. He began to understand why he acted in self - destructive ways, and how to change his behavior in response to the pain.

After a week passed, he knew it was time to meditate again. He found it much easier this time to relax. In his meditation he met his eagle in the meadow. The eagle again beckoned for him to follow. David followed the eagle on a difficult trail leading up a mountain side. He was curious about where they were going.

The eagle and David wound their way up to the top of the mountain where they could look over the valley. The view was breathtaking. The sky was a sharp beautiful blue; the sun was shining, and the breeze was cool, crisp and clear. David again found a rock to sit beside, and began to doze off entering into an altered state.

David felt the sun warming his face, when an angel appeared to him. He couldn't look directly at the angel. What he could perceive didn't match what he had imagined an angel to be. The angel had slanted eyes that glowed with golden light. He was huge in stature with powerful wings. More than anything, David sensed the angel's power and love and felt his body relax even more. The angel told David he was the Archangel Michael, and that he'd been sent by the Higher Power for healing.

David wanted to know more about the angel and began to ask him questions. Archangel Michael told him that he had come to take little David to the light to be healed, but first he had to ask the adult David if he was ready to receive the gift of healing.

David took his time and thought it over carefully. It would mean letting go of little David, a part of his very self. He did want little David to be healed, and knew it would be selfish to keep him. He knew little David had suffered a lot and was sad and tired of living in fear, and fighting for survival.

He decided to give Archangel Michael permission to take little David. Archangel Michael nodded his head with a compassionate smile and wrapped his beautiful wings around little David. Big David said his goodbyes to little David. He told him he loved him and was happy he was going to be healed. Archangel Michael and little David stepped into the white light and disappeared.

David felt good about his decision.

David and his eagle began down the mountainside. The eagle soared with power and strength. He had a satisfied smile knowing little David would be well. David was happy he could visit the eagle any time. He knew life was going to be all right. He no longer had to live in fear and shame.

Allie

Allie walked into the door of my office at Golden Heart Hypnosis. I liked her immediately. She was a pretty woman with blond hair. Every hair was in place, and her clothes were perfectly fitted. She told me she desperately needed to lose weight. In my opinion, she may have been only ten or twenty pounds overweight.

As Allie and I got to know each other better, she told me she was a director at her church. Allie was the "go to" person there. She memorized every detail about the people and church; she was a walking historian and she did it perfectly. Some of her church responsibilities were to see to it that everybody had answers to their questions, to organize and host all parties, and to help set up training programs.

As Allie and I worked together, I suspected she might be depressed. I referred her to a therapist while we continued our work together. As I often do in my practice, I gave her the suggestion, "You may choose to allow those things to surface from your subconscious mind that will assist you in achieving your goals, in the way and time that's best for you."

The resourcefulness of the subconscious mind constantly amazes me. I have learned the client knows how to achieve their goals, much better than I could guess.

Perfectionism was a hard taskmaster for Allie. It dominated every aspect of her life, personally and at work. She felt she had to perfectly remember every detail at the church. She also felt she had to have the perfect house and marriage. Her words were, "I feel like I'm all dried up. I'm so exhausted. I am so ashamed that I just don't have the energy to do things like I used to do."

During the first two hypnosis sessions, she learned to be comfortable with hypnosis while we worked on weight loss. In the third hypnosis session, I asked Allie to start the process of deep breathing and when she was relaxed, I asked her to use her creative imagination and visualize herself someplace safe, someplace where she felt secure.

Allie saw herself swinging on the front porch of her childhood home. She liked it there. Sitting on the swing made her think of her dad, and she loved her dad with all her heart.

I asked Allie if she knew why she had come to that house, and she replied, "I think there's something inside we have to see." I asked her if she would like to go inside the house and she replied, "Yes, I think I would." I asked her how old she was; she told me she was five.

She walked in the house, all dressed up in her favorite dress with matching shoes and socks, and a flawless hair bow.

Quickly, the scene changed and she saw her mother being taken off in an ambulance to the hospital. She was afraid; she didn't know what had happened. Her grandmother told her, "You have to be quiet; you have to be a perfect little girl." She wondered if her mommy was going to the hospital because she had done something that wasn't "perfect". "It's my fault my mommy is sick," she thought to herself. She felt all alone.

Later, Allie saw her mother coming home from the hospital, and her grandmother again told her, "You have to be very quiet. Your mother is sick, and you have to be very still and quiet. You have to be a perfect little girl." She knew her mother's health and happiness were dependent on her being perfect.

After the scene played out in the hypnosis session, I gave Allie the opportunity to process her information. We ended the session with Allie reorienting herself to the room calm, comfortable and relaxed.

This session was one of discovery for Allie, as she realized her inner child carried a wound that was driving her adult life. At five years old her childhood ended as she was driven by the pressing need to be perfect.

Allie has now transitioned into a part-time position at her church, has learned that it's okay not to be perfect, and she is now focusing on enjoying her life.

Comments from Allie: "Working with hypnosis has allowed me a self-awareness level that I've never experienced before. I was able to understand that my desire for perfectionism was causing me pressure and giving me unrealistic goals and expectations of myself.

The knowledge that my perfectionism was no longer driving my life, gave me a new sense of freedom and possibility. Always needing to be perfect locks you in a dark place. It drains you of enjoyment of anything you achieve, because you're always thinking that you should have done it better, even when you created a wonderful product to begin with.

I'm grateful to be rid of that burden, and to understand the pain of the soul in a new way, I can use the newly found awareness to help other people.

Once you experience your own pain, and are aware of what it's done to your life, you go beyond the pain and have a new way of looking at life. You not only have more energy, but I believe you also have more compassion for the pain and suffering of others. This deepened understanding can be used to help people move closer to a place in life where they can focus on their possibilities."

♥ ♥ ♥

I Always Believe I'm in Trouble

Twice this week I've heard the statement, *I always believe I'm in trouble*, so I started thinking about why people are not be able to shake off this feeling. I began to realize the wounds of the inner child are often at the root of these feelings. In instances where the inner child has received continual criticism or abuse, the inner child believes he/she is in trouble all the time, whether or not they are. The same belief pervades their adult life. Believing you're in trouble all the time can often be accompanied by guilt.

Most people occasionally experience guilt with introspection playing a healthy role in correcting poor behavior. However, toxic guilt is one of the byproducts of continual criticism and abuse. Do you believe you are in trouble all the time? Do you feel guilty about everything you say and do?

Releasing the hold guilt has on you, can be life changing. You can accomplish this by developing realistic expectations for yourself, giving yourself respect and forgiveness, and clarifying the expectations of other relationships in your life.

Where do your expectations of yourself come from? Are they from within, or are you responding to pressure to meet others expectations of you? You and the people around you will benefit greatly - when you resist the desire to satisfy others expectations, at your own expense.

When your actions and behaviors are guilt free, you become more authentic. Also, when you stop doing things for others out of guilt, you give them the gift being responsible for their own choices and actions. This opens the door for positive changes in your relationships.

Victim Mentality

Have you ever asked yourself, "Why does this always have to happen to me?" I know I frequently did while I was going through life with a daughter suffering from addiction. The victim mentality involves blame, guilt and shame. The victim says, "Poor me." Staying in the victim mentality is an easy thing to do, particularly if somebody has treated you poorly, or if you have suffered at the hands of others. The victim tells you, "I'm not good enough." "I'm not intelligent enough." "I'm not attractive enough." "I can't do that."

Sometimes when bad things happen, you become frozen in reaction to those bad things. Bad things happen to everyone. What is important is how you choose to respond to those bad things. Your job is to live a happy life expressing kindness and a loving heart.

People stay in victimhood by defending the ego, listening to negative self talk, and by making poor relationship choices. Abuse is usually caused by others actions; but the victim generally believes they have no control over any part of their life.

The ego is like a two year old; "it's all about me, me, me." It is capable of throwing tantrums to control its environment, particularly if it gets the attention it desires. It always wants to believe it is in charge and cannot see any perspective except its own.

The ego also wants to feel important and it doesn't care how it goes about it, so long as it makes you feel and look good. It wants you to believe your life's situation is everyone else's fault; therefore, you don't have to be held responsible because you are the victim.

Not only does the ego sometimes hold you in victimhood but negative self talk also supports the role of the victim. It allows you to view your situation through a distorted lens, causing you to see a false reality. Distorted beliefs create fixed and limiting thinking, which are hard to overcome. Distortions fog your decision-making ability, and lead you to bad decisions, more pain and malfunction. A vicious cycle is: Bad decisions/I am a victim/ I am a victim/Bad decisions.

Confronting your negativity and limiting beliefs can help you step out of victimhood so that you can live a passionate and full life.

Living a life of victimhood usually impacts your relationships. Remember, when you put out a specific energy, it attracts like energy. Negative comments from other people can cause you to become negative, making it easy to misinterpret what others say to you. Being around negative people is infectious and spreads like flu in a hospital. It starts with one person's negative words, which then infects many people.

If you have a negative mentality, you will just accept what others say and do without evaluation. Word is like seed. Put it in fertile ground and it will flourish; put the seed in barren ground and it wither up and die. The human mind is extremely fertile; the only problem is that, too often, it is fertile for seeds of negativity.

Do you believe bad things always happen to you, or do you think you are responsible for your life and what happens to you? Victimhood is perpetuated by taking what other people say and do personally. It's not what is said that hurts you. No one can make another do, think or feel something. What really hurts you is what they say touches your personal wound.

It is your responsibility to stay centered regardless of other people's words. You can respond to others without anger and frustration by remembering what others say and do is about them, not you. You have the freedom to choose to love yourself and others. Loving yourself keeps energy moving through your body in a positive way.

Forgiveness can release you from being a victim all your life. Sometimes forgiveness needs to extend beyond forgiving others, to forgiving yourself, and to forgiving God, as well. We often carry grudges for years, which make us feel entitled to our resentment.

Being unwilling to forgive hurts you more than it hurts others. It causes a hole in your soul, leaving you open to dark energy attachments, which can imprison you to negativity and depression. Being a victim can make your inner child hide in the dark as we will see in the next story.

> Self-pity in its early stages is as snug as a feather mattress. Only when it hardens does it become uncomfortable.
>
> ~Maya Angelo

♥ ♥ ♥

Lily

Lily had been abused when she was little. She was sad, frightened and angry. She hid in the dark and never came out to play. Occasionally, she came out when somebody made her frightened or angry, but no one knew when she was there. She would go back to the dark as quickly as she came out, so that no one could hurt her. It was lonely in the dark, but she felt safe there; even though she longed to come out to play like other children.

One night, Lily had a dream that she was walking down a long hallway with a light at the end of it. Bravely, she tiptoed up to the light and saw a beautiful shinning white house with a pretty woman standing on the porch. Lily pulled back in the dark to hide. She so much wanted to speak to the woman. She took a small timid step into the light. The woman on the porch gave Lily a huge smile and told her, "I've been waiting for you to come out of your darkness so that I could talk to you."

The woman seemed very nice, but Lily didn't trust anyone just yet. She ran back into her dark corner, which now seemed even more lonesome.

She soon dreamed about the pretty lady again. Curiosity was getting the best of Lily. She wondered who this woman was, and why she kept dreaming of her. When she thought of her, she began to hope that perhaps the lady could someday take her out of the darkness. The lady seemed so loving; she could see her golden heart.

The next night Lily found herself dreaming again; she was again in a long corridor walking toward the light. This time it was easy to find her way to the white house.

Arriving at the house, Lily could see the woman with the golden heart, but decided to hide in the shadows until she felt safe. The pretty woman looked directly at Lily. How could she know she was there hiding? When the pretty lady walked over to her, Lily was so scared she almost retreated to her dark corner.

The lady said her name was Amber. Surprising herself, she found the courage to speak to the lady saying, "My name is Lily. I was named after my grandmother."

Amber began telling Lily she knew what she had experienced, especially the pain and loneliness. She even knew that Lily had been hiding in the dark corner. Amber explained to the little girl that she wanted to be a loving parent to Lily. Lily so much wanted to be hugged and held, but she was too frightened to allow anyone close to her.

The dark was a familiar place.

Little Lily had another dream. Instantly, she moved toward the door of the house and to Amber. Lily kept wondering why she was being drawn to the white house. When she arrived, Amber was waiting for her on the porch in her rocker. This time Lily came out of the dark and up onto the porch. Amber told Lily she could be her mother, and she would love her with all her heart.

Amber held out her arms to Lily, picked her up and onto her lap. It felt so good to be happy, and to be held, yet tears began to flow. Lily remembered someone had been cruel to her, and the crying helped the pain flow out. She knew she was safe, and let go. Amber told her over and over that everything was going to be all right. She told her what a beautiful girl she was and told her that it was wonderful to hold her in her arms. Lily became very quiet and calm. She decided to stay at the house with Amber.

One day Lily saw another child playing in the yard next to her house and asked Amber if she could go play with the child. Amber agreed, and kept an eye on the children from the front porch. After the children played awhile, Lily came to Amber and asked if her new friend could come to stay with them.

Amber took Lily in her arms and explained that it was okay for her to play with the child, but her new friend would have to go back to her own house. Amber explained to Lily you have to take your time to really let the friendship grow if you want your relationship to last.

When little Lily couldn't convince Amber to let her friend stay, she began to throw a tantrum, stomping her feet and shouting, "I hate you! "Amber let Lily know that she was the parent and would make adult decisions which were best for both children. Lily didn't like it much, but knew Amber was right. Time passed and Amber and Lily got to know each other better. Lily knew she could trust Amber to make adult decisions that were best for her.

Amber knew it was time to go home where she now lives as an adult and she asked Lily if she would like to go home with her. Lily shook her head yes. Amber took her hand. She then let Lily step into her heart where they would always be together.

Amber and Lily sat in a beautiful garden, near a stream where the sun shined and butterflies landed on the flowers. The adult Amber heard a small voice say, "I love you." Amber smiled and Lily knew she was loved.

Soul Exercise 10: Love Your Inner Child

Always do meditation in a relaxing, private place. You may tape record this meditation and play it back.

(Change the gender to correspond to your gender type.)

Focus your eyes on a spot on the ceiling, staring at it until the muscles around your eyes become tired. Close your eyes and breathing deeply, hold your breath for seven counts. Then breathe out for seven counts and hold for seven counts. Breathe in for seven counts and hold your breath for seven counts, and then breathe out seven counts. Do three repetitions of breathing and counting. As you count, imagine yourself breathing out all of the tension in your body, completely emptying your lungs.

On the last in - breath of the last set, hold your breath as long as you can. Then imagine there is a white light above your head and pull the light down into your body. Let it filter all the way down to the tips of your toes, and then breathe out. Imagine that you're exhaling stress out of your toes . . . . Breathe in, feeling the air against your nostrils. Let the air go deeply into your lungs while expanding and holding, and then breathe out again.

Use your imagination, and visualize that you're in a meadow. You can see beautiful green grass; it smells like springtime . . . . The sun is shining on your body and you can feel warmth soaking into your hair, into your face, into your hands and into your feet. The warmth is adding to your relaxation . . . .

You feel so very incredibly relaxed and you hear a bird singing. You notice it is an unusual bird; its song is beautiful music to your ears. Become aware of the beautiful flowers planted in the meadow; their bright colors dance in the breeze. As their fragrance drifts up to your nose, you breathe deeply. You feel nature comforting you and surrounding you with a beauty that mystifies you . . . .

You ask your inner child to join you in the garden. As you look up, you see your inner child quietly standing in your garden. She is shy and looks lonely. You pick a flower and give it as a gift to your inner child. You let her know that you are a friend, and invite her to sit down beside you. You sit together in comfortable silence.

You both notice a beautiful butterfly with colorful wings sparkling in the sun, and dancing in the breeze. The butterfly flies from flower to flower; then crawls up to the very center of one of the flowers to sip nectar. Your inner child is fascinated and enchanted as she watches. Your inner child smiles as you take her by the hand, and walk close to the flower and the butterfly. The two of you watch as the butterfly lands on your hand. This mysterious and beautiful gesture brings you and your inner child closer, touching your hearts.

A healing takes place for the two of you. All fears and worries melt away, and in their place is peace and contentment . . . .

You ask the inner child if she would like to enter into the garden of your heart. You explain that she will be protected and safe with you. She agrees. You take the child in your hands and lift her up; she melts into your heart. Here she can live the bright, beautiful, creative life that she always wanted. You tell her that you love her more than anything in the world, and that you want her to stay with you, and that the universe wants her to stay, too. You tell her how very good and beautiful she is.

Before you leave this time and place, you give your inner child a special gift, that will touch her heart and make her smile. She receives the gift. Promise her you will always listen to what she has to say, and you will ask her to come out to play. Remind her that she has done nothing wrong . . . . As you leave this place, you smile, put your feet on the ground, open your eyes and return to a normal state of awareness.

6
Broken Hearts

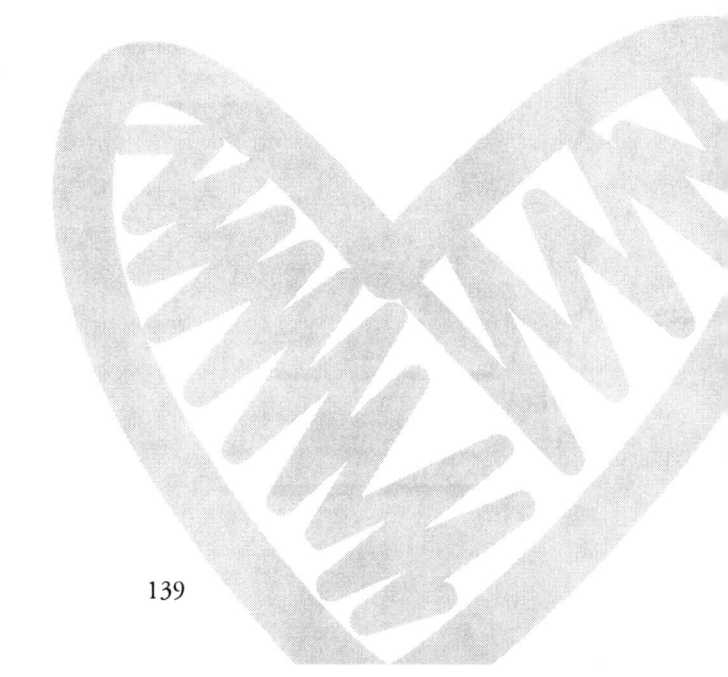

Conflict

~Sharron Magyar

There's a battle going on between the head and the heart,
My brain tells me what to do from the start.
The problem is it leaves a crying heart.
If I follow my heart there will be more pain;
Conflict out of this argument, I can't trust my sentiment.
If I follow my heart, my brain never stops questioning.
If I follow my brain, my heart never stops breaking.
So how do I balance the equation?
I can be convicted out of my own ineptitude;
Choose heart; maybe pay a big price.
Choose brain, the cost is only an empty heart.
Around and around with no solution,
Heart and brain standing diametrically apart.

My heart ran through the gamut of emotions living life with a daughter who was suffering from addiction. I had an angry heart, a broken heart, and a grieving heart. Heart wounds are extremely painful and I didn't think I was going to survive them. People don't think too much about their heart if they have a happy heart. If they have a wounded heart they think about it all the time. The mind and emotions cannot disconnect from a damaged heart.

Normally, emotions that rule the heart bring compassion, softness, and truth into your life. However when the heart is carrying a wound, emotions gets stuck and can be difficult to heal. Hurt, anger and despair can become locked in your heart. Unresolved emotions bring disharmonious energy into your relationships.

This disharmonious energy often is connected to emotional experiences which can cause repeated negative life events. These experiences can injure the heart and cause feelings of abandonment. A child will feel abandonment if they hear the words, "I wanted a boy rather than a girl," (or visa-versa) at birth. The child adopts the belief that "no one wants me." Abandonment causes the heart to feel empty and alone.

Have you ever known anyone who continually moves from relationship to relationship? Chances are good they experienced early abandonment at birth. They are acting out their heart belief in their physical reality. Until the heart is healed of its early abandonment issues, it will be difficult to form a healthy relationship with anyone.

Another example of a heart wound that filters down to the subconscious occurs when a parent continually criticizes a child. Through implied actions or direct words, the child could develop a mistaken belief that he is a failure. Mistaken beliefs accepted by the heart often lead to self harm.

If you carry a heart wound through many years, you can still find yourself wondering why you feel empty, depressed, and stuck in life. The age old adage that time heals wounds is not always appropriate. Heart patterns repeated throughout a person's life bring attention to wounds in the subconscious waiting to be healed.

Most of our daily functions are driven by the condition of our heart, yet many people fear going to the root of their heart problems. A sad, grieving, broken heart makes you feel emotions deeply. You have to grieve in order to move on. By going through the intense pain, you will eventually surface as a stronger person ready to tackle problems head on. Soon pain loses its stronghold over you.

Allowing yourself to experience a broken heart can lead to fearlessness, which can be a source of power. If you're not aware of your emotions, you cannot live with authenticity, richness, and fullness of life. Ask yourself what is the condition of your heart? Stay with the emotions which surface to release heart wounds.

> Love is never lost. If not reciprocated, it will flow back and soften and purify the heart.
>
> ~Washington Irving

Soul Exercise 11: Open Your Heart

Always do meditation in a relaxing, private place. You may tape record this meditation and play it back.

- ♥ Take a deep breath. Breathe deeply into your belly for seven counts; hold your breath for seven counts; exhale for seven counts, and hold for seven counts. Repeat this process seven times. Focus on releasing all the negativity while exhaling. Breathe in tranquility and peace as you inhale. Breathe out stress and tension as you exhale. Eventually, you will step into a natural breathing rhythm and fall into a deep relaxation.

- When you are completely relaxed, call forward the deepest part of yourself to help heal your heart, and free you from the wounds of the past. Allow yourself to connect with your feelings of emptiness and sadness. Visualize your heart in your mind's eye while connecting to your feelings.

- Your heart may appear as having holes in it, as having a tear in it, or even appear to be split in two. Mobilize all your healing forces and imagine a golden light within your heart. Allow the golden light to surround your heart while it is healing it. Permeate the heart completely with the golden light, filling in all the holes, repairing all the tears or splits. Imagine yourself letting go of all the harmful ways you have tried to fill the holes in the past which caused you grief. Feel love and healing entering your heart. Notice that your heart is free to love.

- Thank the deepest part of yourself for the freedom it has given you to be filled with love. Count up to five and return to normal awareness. Each night before you fall asleep visualize your gold filled heart.

Addicted to Love

Joan came to Golden Heart Hypnosis because she wanted to reduce her stress. As I did her interview she shared that she had just terminated a relationship in which she experienced "love at first sight." Joan just knew that James was the one. Soon into the relationship, Joan recognized she didn't particularly like James's friends. She did everything she could to fit into his group, even though they were shallow and treated her callously. Looking back, she couldn't believe that she'd given up so much of herself to be in a relationship.

While Joan was with James, her obsession with him took over her life. She stopped showing up for family functions; dropped all of her friends; and acted self-absorbed around her co-workers. To the people who loved her, it was as if Joan had fallen off the face of the earth.

Joan was giving everything in the relationship and James was taking. What Joan couldn't understand was why she thought he really loved her. In the beginning, it seemed that everything was perfect. Shortly after James told Joan that he loved her with all his heart and soul, he picked a fight and created uproar. He then told Joan he didn't know if he wanted to be with her or not.

Joan was struggling with feelings of fear, loneliness, abandonment and rejection. She had heard the saying, "she died of a broken heart." She felt like she was dying. She did everything she could to get him back. She knew she was walking on eggshells around him and his friends. Along with his need to have more space, she found herself doing a dance centering on his need to have control of the schedule.

He just wouldn't seem to let her in, and Joan didn't know what she'd done wrong.

Joan was a teacher, smart and attractive, with lots of friends. How did everything get off track for her, and why did she lose her sense of individuality? She knew if she allowed the relationship to go further, it had the potential to develop into an abusive situation. Joan's goal with hypnosis was to work on self-esteem and stress management.

We started a series of sessions designed to create a more positive outlook on life. What I love about hypnosis is that each person has the answer within themselves for meeting their goals, and the perfect timing for retrieving meaningful memories. My job, as a consulting hypnotist, is to support her in her *self*-healing.

First session: We began with a Shamanic exercise in which I helped her detach the cords connecting their hearts, and then she retrieved her soul part that she had given to James. We ended the session by surrounding him with the white light of love. I then gave Joan suggestions of self-love.

Session two and three: We worked on ego strengthening. I gave Joan suggestions that she would have more energy, be much less easily tired, and much less easily discouraged. I also gave her the suggestion that she could rely on herself and her own judgment. Joan was also practicing self-hypnosis to become more relaxed and less stressed each day. Self-hypnosis allowed her to make her own hypnosis suggestions according to her personal goals.

Fourth session: At this point in our work together, Joan had become accomplished and comfortable with hypnosis as well as self-hypnosis. We started our session with some deep breathing and relaxing imagery. It didn't take long for her to become inwardly focused while connecting with her subconscious mind. I asked her if she could give herself permission to go to the place giving her the most problem at this time in her life which would assist her in achieving her goals. She nodded her head yes. I had no idea where that might be.

I counted her back into the new place, and asked her where she was. She said she was standing by the door of her sister's bedroom. I asked her what she was doing. She said she was watching.

"How old are you, Joan?" I asked.

Joan replied, "Two."

"Why are you at your sister's bedroom door Joan?"

"I want my sis to play with me, but she can't get out of bed. I want my mommy, but my mommy told me, "Not now, I have to take care of your sister." Joan tells me she feels funny in her stomach, and she misses her mommy and her sister. She grabs her "blankie" and sits in the corner by herself; she is lonely and needs a hug.

I gave Joan's inner child suggestions of love and comfort before she was reoriented to the here and now.

Joan's Comments:

I remember spending a lot of time by myself when I was growing up. I had a sister who was in a bad accident, and was bedridden for a long time. Our family life revolved around taking care of my older sister.

It took a while for me to recognize the importance of the fourth hypnosis session. Eventually, I connected with my feelings of loneliness and abandonment as a two-year-old. I began to see how I've taken those feelings that were unexplainable to me as a child into my adulthood.

I now recognize when feelings of loneliness and abandonment step up, they come from the two year old. I can now choose to observe the feelings, rather than react to them and reassure my inner child she is loved.

I'm spending more time thinking about what I want in a relationship, and I am recognizing I have to keep my sense of self. The main thing that I'm working on is letting relationships develop and grow, rather than jumping right into them.

> I don't take relationships too seriously, but everyone else seems to. And when you get your heart broken, it's like the end of the world. And I look at it as that was one moment in your life, one chapter. That person helped you grow and figure out what kind of person you want to be with in the future.
>
> ~Colbie Caillat

Soul Exercise 12: Engage in Your Feelings

When you're feeling stuck and you are unable to take action, bring your awareness to your body and notice the part of you that is resisting action. Compassionately listen to the part of yourself that needs to have a voice. What does the feeling part of you want you to know? Get to know your feeling; give it words and images.

You may be amazed at what comes up. Give yourself time to cycle your feelings through until you have awareness and resolution.

Lonely Heart

The other day I was watching a TV show in which a woman was talking online to men, pretending that she was an under-aged girl. She would invite them into her house for sex; her true purpose was to entrap pedophiles. Once the men were caught, the show's announcer asked if they had seen his show before, and if they had been concerned about walking into a trap? Many of the men replied yes, they had seen the show on TV, and, yes, they were concerned about getting caught.

Here was the complicated part; they came regardless of their fears. The men were from all walks of life. They were married; they were servicemen; they were professionals; they were truck drivers, etc. The commentator asked why they came anyway? Surprisingly, the most common answer they gave was that they were lonely.

What exactly is loneliness? It's a feeling of worthlessness, emptiness, a lack of control and ultimately, a threat to oneself. Loneliness affects the self-identity.

John Cacioppo from the University of Chicago spent many years studying the effects of loneliness. His studies established an immediate biological connection between being lonely and ill health. Loneliness is tied to hardening of the arteries, problems with learning and memory, and inflammation in the body. It often damages the quality of sleep, which negatively affects a person both physically and psychologically.

Loneliness also can have a negative social impact on a person. It can be the driving force that keeps many people in abusive relationships. Lonely people can spend hours on the internet, tolerate friends they don't like, spend a lifetime looking for that special one, grieve indefinitely, and still be lonely. They can even be lonely in a room full of people.

Some of the greatest minds of history have experienced extreme loneliness connected with spiritual, emotional or physical situations. Eventually their ability to undergo loneliness led them to accept remarkable life challenges and changes leading them to discoveries and transformation. Milton Erickson, Isaac Newton, and Judy Garland readily come to my mind.

The positive thing about loneliness is that it can be a signal to change something in your life. Do you need to reach out to cultivate new relationships? Do you need to weed out relationships that are not healthy for you? Do you need to do personal work on improving yourself? Embracing loneliness can lead to greater understanding of yourself and others.

Loneliness has different guises and faces. I know that when my daughter was at the height of her addiction, my husband Steve and I felt lonely. Where were the feelings of loneliness coming from?

Loneliness is often created through self imposed walls that prevent a person from receiving and giving love. On the surface the wall does prevent hurt from entering in, but it also prevents love from entering.

Making a conscious choice to let down protective walls takes courage. My mother has a saying. "It doesn't have to feel good to be good for you." There is a lifetime of wisdom in those words. Through our experience of loneliness, Steve and I discovered there were many avenues of growth available to us. We learned that giving what we wanted to receive had huge rewards.

The key to rising above a lonely heart is to have a loving heart.

> It is strange to be known so universally and yet to be lonely.
>
> ~Albert Einstein

Soul Exercise 13: Healing Loneliness

Always do meditation in a relaxing, private place. You may tape record this meditation and play it back.

- ♥ *Take a deep breath. Breathe deeply into your belly for seven counts; hold your breath for seven counts; exhale for seven counts, and hold for seven counts. Repeat this process seven times. Focus on releasing all the negativity while exhaling. Breathe in tranquility and peace as you inhale. Breathe out stress and tension as you exhale. Eventually, you will step into a natural breathing rhythm and fall into a deep relaxation.*

- ♥ *As you relax allow every muscle to become loose and limp. . . . Just let go of everything . . . . Enjoy relaxing . . . . And maybe you can imagine lying in the sun . . . . And in the sky there are clouds drifting across the sky.... And you can imagine yourself in a cloud.... Feel your body becoming lighter.... You feel yourself gently supported.... Floating and drifting.... Feel it rising and carrying you up into the sky.... While the cloud is snuggled up against your skin.*

❤ *Expand your awareness to see down below.... Absorb the sunlight.... Feel the weight of your body being supported and ask yourself the source of loneliness in your life.... Then ask what you can do to alleviate or resolve the loneliness. Consider the matter for a few moments and then count to five bringing your awareness into the room.*

Tomorrow

~Sharron Magyar

Tomorrow I'll do better than I did today.

I'll go that extra mile, be thoughtful in every way.

I'll show you that I love you,

Have time to kiss and hug you;

Give a loving embrace; tell you what you've meant to me.

If I'm not careful, tomorrow will be just like yesterday.

You're untouchable; no one can ever hurt you again.

A wall up so high, I don't even know where to begin.

Your armor you'll wear so you can't feel guilt or pain;

A path of destruction you spread with all your pain,

A wall up locking in your heart, invincible,

Indefensible and impenetrable to the end.

Tomorrow just another day.

> God gave you a gift of 86,400 seconds today. Have you used one to say "thank you?"
>
> ~William A. Ward

Gratitude

I had to laugh when I gave out an assignment to people participating in a workshop at my office. During the following week they were to write down every time they thought something negative. Boy, did everyone come back the next week with all kinds of surprises. One of the participants said, "I couldn't believe how many times I said something negative to my husband, and I really love my husband." It's so easy to say negative things about other people when you are in a relationship.

My husband and I have been married for forty-six years. I have given considerable thought about what's made our relationship enduring. Heaven knows we've had huge trials in our lifetime. We lived through our daughter's addiction. Steve had quadruple bypass surgery and a stroke. I was run over by a car, while I was walking down the street. Through it all, I have been grateful for our relationship, and we each try to express it in a million ways. It would have been easy to drop down into the abyss of victimhood and blame everyone, including God, for our circumstances.

Whether it's a friendship, a parent-child relationship, or a lover-spouse relationship, why is gratitude so important? A grateful mind is constantly fixed on the positive; therefore, it will attract the positive. Gratitude is important because it has a high-energy vibration; it can elevate, as well as keep you on a higher energetic level.

What stands in the way of gratitude in relationships? Many of us go through life stuck in the idea that things should be a certain way. There are no accidents in our relationships. Every situation that looks bad has a good side, if you look for it. Sometimes you have to take the 'good' on faith, and wait until enough time passes for it to become apparent.

What was the 'good' when my husband had bypass surgery and a stroke? He learned to take better care of his health and live in the moment. What was the 'good' when I was walking down the street and was hit by a car? I learned about many different alternative healing modalities along with traditional methods, as well as how trauma is imprinted on the subconscious mind. What was the 'good' from my daughter being addicted to drugs? I learned that I can't control life or what others think and do; I can only choose how to respond to life.

There were a million other 'goods,' but to me the most evident good is that it gave me passion to write and help people heal from wounds. The lows in my life helped me to learn to live life mindfully and to be in the moment. I also learned the value of having forgiveness in my heart.

The 'good' is in the choices we make while we respond to the 'bad'.

Gratitude can grow out of the ashes of life.

> Everything can be taken from a man or a woman but one thing: The last of human freedoms to choose one's attitude in any given set of circumstances, to choose one's own way.
>
> ~Viktor Frankl

Soul Exercise 14: Opening to Gratitude

Always do meditation in a relaxing, private place. You may tape record this meditation and play it back.

- 💚 *Do deep breathing exercises and enter into a relaxed state. When you are deeply relaxed, reflect on events that you are grateful for, that happened throughout the day. These do not have to be big things. They could be as simple as, "I am grateful someone made me coffee." Or, "I am grateful for the sunrise." Especially in your worst day, it is important to experience gratefulness in your heart. Your challenge is to practice a daily habit of focusing on gratitude.*

- *Next, as you continue to reflect on the day, think about the events that you were able to do that you are grateful for. They can be simple things to you. For example, I am grateful I can walk today, and I am grateful I have exercised today. Hold the thoughts of gratefulness in your mind as you bring your awareness back into the room. A grateful heart draws more things into your life to be grateful about.*

- *After your meditation, make a gratitude collage by gathering pictures of things you are grateful for. Paste the pictures on a poster board. Put the collage where you will see it daily, and keep the collage updated. You will be surprised at the things you find to add to the board.*

Detachment

How many times do you find yourself saying and doing things that hurt yourself and others? Put your foot in your mouth? Afterwards, you relive the events in your mind and obsess emotionally. You kick yourself over and over again. Having a daughter addicted to drugs was a challenge, and I found myself emotionally involved against my will and better judgment. I got angry, frustrated and disappointed. There were highs and there were lows, but mostly lows.

Each time a catastrophe came, I swore I'd stay cool and calm. Each time I'd forget, and fall into an emotional tornado of despair. I knew detaching from the emotional devastation of my daughter's addiction was a matter of self-survival. I just didn't know how to do it. My quandary – find a way to detach without being an unloving parent. It took years of struggle and a lot of tears, but I finally figured it out.

I realized that I could ask myself the question, "If I take action, will it prevent my daughter from getting a lesson she should be getting on her own?" If the answer to that question was "yes," I would stop myself from taking action. If the answer was "no", I could give myself permission to take action.

What I'm talking about are life circumstances and behaviors over which you have no control. What is your reaction to them? You say to yourself, "I'm so angry, because he/she did that," or "they shouldn't have treated me that way." Sometimes you can't change what happens in your life; you can only control your response to it. It took me a long time to realize that I could not change my daughter's addiction, and accept all I could control was my reaction.

Inevitably, 'bad' things will happen on life's journey. Our challenge is to focus on staying balanced and centered through it all. Experiencing the 'bad' provides you with the opportunity to learn love and discernment.

Do you struggle with being overly attached in relationships? Is your life controlled by your emotional involvement? Do you believe your happiness depends on others? Energy is wasted on anger, frustration, unhappiness, disappointments and fights and expecting the person you're in a relationship with will change? Do you value others' thoughts and feelings more than you value your own opinion of yourself?

There are numerous ways to detach from your need to control other people and their behaviors. You have a right to experience peace and harmony, and your peacefulness can not be contingent on another's actions and behavior. (That took me about fifty years to understand.)

Meditation and self-hypnosis allow you to detach emotionally from your situation. Being conscious of your breath can help you instantly relax. An easy way to cycle stuck energy is to exercise as it puts you in touch with your body. Visualizing positive outcomes to stressful situations that previously raised anger and agitation helps you respond differently. Draw on your personal resources to help you cope with times that seem negative. Choose your reaction!

Soul Exercise 15: Walking Mindfully

The goal is to be totally in the moment with walking. As you become more practiced you will find opportunities for information to float up from your subconscious mind.

- ❤ You can walk mindfully anyplace; all you have to do is set your intention to connect to your surrounding and your thoughts, feelings and sensation.

- ❤ Focus your attention on your feet. Feel them hit the ground as you begin to walk. Notice the muscles in your legs. How do they feel? What muscles contract and lengthen? Notice where you step and the quality of your steps. Direct your attention on the ground beneath your feet.

- ❤ Engage all of your senses to your surroundings. What do you see, hear, smell, taste and feel? Feel the sun and air on your skin? What do you see around you?

- ♥ Expand you awareness to include how you are feeling inside. What are you thinking, what are you feeling? Are your thoughts and emotions extreme or are they mild? Do you think your thoughts are good or bad or are you unbiased about them? Just practice the art of observation.

Set your intention to practice every day.

Sherry

Sherry came to the door of Golden Heart Hypnosis seeking a more positive attitude in life. As we got into the conversation about her life, she told me that she had two children, a twenty - three year old daughter, and a son that was nineteen. She was frustrated because her daughter just couldn't seem to make the transition to living on her own. I'll bet many people reading this can instantly identify with the situation. Adult children living at home seem to be more prevalent in today's society.

Sherry shared with me the story of her little daughter being hospitalized at around two years old. She almost died. It had been a rocky road with her infant's health. Sherry loved her daughter with all her heart and soul.

As we began hypnosis, Sherry sat in the chair and listened to my voice as I guided her to release her stress. I saw her breath deepen and drop into an even rhythm as she entered into a deep state of relaxation. Her shoulders relaxed, and Sherry became still and silent.

I asked Sherry if she was comfortable and cozy, and she replied, "Yes." Next, I asked her, "Would you be at ease with using your imagination to call your daughter to you?" She replied, "Yes." She set the intention to call her daughter to herself and visualized her standing in front of her. (Many people can visualize during hypnosis, others don't. There is no right or wrong. It's similar to having different learning modalities).

I next asked Sherry to examine herself and her daughter to see if there were cords going to either of them. She could visualize a cord going from her daughter's heart to her heart. Sherry recognized she had given her daughter a part of the energy of her soul when she was very ill.

I asked Sherry if she could give herself permission to call her soul part back. She said she'd have to think if that was in her best interest. After giving it some thought, she decided to retrieve her soul part. At the same time I sent love from my golden heart to her daughter's heart to fill up the space where her mother's soul part had been residing. I then gave Sherry some positive posthypnotic suggestions and counted her up to normal waking awareness.

Later, I explained that although the soul exchange was well intentioned, her daughter could not use another person's soul energy. I shared with Sherry that her daughter would experience the extra soul energy as a burden, and that Sherry would feel lost energy from the missing soul part.

Sherry's Comments:

"I recognized my daughter, Rebecca, was stuck in her life and she couldn't make the separation from me that was necessary for her to move into adulthood. One part of me wanted to hold on to her. The mature part of me knew it was healthy for my daughter to move into a more independent life.

The hypnosis session started a change in our relationship. We have now moved into a more adult relationship. Rebecca moved out of the house three months ago to start her adult life."

We do many things both consciously and subconsciously out of love, that do not always benefit us.

Zachary

Zachary was a cute little boy; he had dark curly hair with big blue eyes. He loved to go for walks among the trees and grass. The wind blew through the leaves to sing a beautiful song; it made him feel free. One day, he was going for a walk at the wildlife sanctuary. It was his favorite place because he could find frogs, grasshoppers, worms and butterflies. He could hear the birds singing and he could see the flowers dancing in the breeze. If he was very, very, very careful, he might find a frog, mouse or a turtle.

What Zachary really liked most of all about walking the paths were the songs he heard. He heard the birds singing, the crickets chirping, the owl hooting, even the song of the grass while it blew in the wind. He thought it all sounded so pretty.

One day as he was walking in the woods, he began to feel very, very sad. Tears started dropping from his eyes. He just couldn't explain the feeling that he had in his body; all he knew was that his heart couldn't sing because of the sadness he felt. The animals of the forest were observant and they noticed his sadness. A rabbit hopped up to Zachary and asked him what he was so sad about? "Why are you crying?"

The little boy replied, "I've lost my song."

The rabbit said, "What do you mean you've lost your song?

The little boy replied, "I've lost my song, I can't sing from my heart like the birds, the flowers, the trees and the grass."

Rabbit called over his forest friends. They gathered to put their heads together; they tried to figure out where the little boy's song had gone. They looked all around the ground and all through the forest. They couldn't find the song from Zachary's heart.

A big hawk swooped up into the sky and looked at him from his high vantage point. All of a sudden, he saw that Zachary's songs were leaking out of his heart and onto the ground. The animals laid the little boy down on the grass; they saw little poisonous arrows sticking out of his heart. His animal friends knew that these were bad. They asked him where the poisonous arrows had come from. The little boy replied they were from his daddy's mean words.

All of the animals had a serious consultation. They decided that they must remove the barbs so that the little boy could keep his song in his heart. The little boy was frightened. He'd had those barbs for a long time. He was scared to remove them now. The animals assured him that they would be gentle and kind while drawing them out. They could do it at Zachary's own pace.

Zachary decided to take a chance, a risk, and make a change, because he wanted so badly to have a song in his heart. He told them, "I'm ready to be healthy and whole with my own song in my heart."

MY GOLDEN HEART PUTTING THE PIECES BACK TOGETHER AGAIN

All the animals gathered around in a circle to give him love and support, while he had the barbs extracted. The owl swooped down and grabbed the barbs with his claws to gently pull them out. The boy felt a little pain, but not as much as he thought there would be. The animals put special herbs on the wounds, and the little boy began to heal slowly but surely.

As time passed, he had to remind himself that he didn't carry those poisonous arrows anymore. When he remembered, it felt very good.

The little boy grew up, often returning to the woods. He sang a song from his heart so that everyone could hear. A beautiful melody it was, and the song touched other people's hearts so they could sing their songs, too.

Heart Songs

A song in the heart

Bringing the sunshine in,

A smile on the face, music within.

Touch another soul with warmth,

A song, beauty and grace.

A song in the heart,

A song of love, a song of joy,

Soothes the soul, a sweet embrace.

A song about peace, a song in the heart

A delight and dance,

A sweet smile

A moment.

7 Family

Stephanie's Story

As a little girl Stephanie, my second daughter, loved and adored her older sister, Tammy. When the girls got into their teen years, Tammy started abusing drugs; Stephanie started feeling the pain of Tammy's addiction. When one child is ill, the siblings in the family are profoundly affected by that illness.

These illnesses could be physical, mental, emotional, or addiction. In the best-case scenario, the siblings will grow with compassion and empathy. In the worst case scenario, the sibling will hold shame and anger in their heart at both the sibling and at the circumstances. Usually there is some level of each.

Embarrassment became the norm for Stephanie, yet she loved her sister with all her heart. I wish I could change what Stephanie endured throughout her childhood. No child should have to worry every day if their sibling is going to live or die.

Addiction is a monster that attracts more monsters, and can drag families down into the depths of despair. As an adult, Stephanie became angry with Tammy for what she was putting Steve and me, and Tammy's children through.

Stephanie's Comments:

"The most difficult thing for me in dealing with a sister who had an addiction was that I couldn't fix it. I couldn't fix it for Tammy and I couldn't fix it for my mom and dad. I could not understand why she just couldn't quit. Didn't she see how it was affecting every single person around her that loved her?

It took me a very long time to realize it wasn't necessarily a conscious choice that she was making, and that it was an illness. I won't lie and say that I do not carry some anger as a result of my sister's addiction, but what I can say is that I've grown a lot and I've learned a lot. I think when something like this happens to you and your family, there are so many things you go through that make you realize just how important family is.

I never take for granted any time that I get to spend with my parents, my husband or my children, because I know just how quickly all that can be taken away. I would say the biggest change in me has been that I used to live to work, I now work to live. Family comes first and always will."

Tammy's Story

I had finally graduated from college; and it was a tough haul. I was tired. After graduation, Steve and I decided to take a well-deserved week off to go camping. We enjoyed fishing out of the boat; Steve fished while I read and slept. We were having much fun just relaxing and hanging around. In the middle of our week, we received a frantic call from our daughter, Stephanie. She felt terrible about calling us, but told us we needed to come home right away. Tammy was in trouble. I knew that if Stephanie was calling, Tammy was in really big trouble.

While her son was gone for the weekend, Tammy and one of her son's fourteen-year-old friend's got high and went to a neighboring town. They broke into a house and stole a bunch of stuff.

The fourteen-year-old was driving the car home. Tammy was so drugged out she couldn't talk, let alone drive. Seeing them weaving on the road back home, the police pulled the car over. Once they saw everything in the back seat that they had stolen from the house, the police arrested them. It later came out that Tammy was having sex with the fourteen-year old boy.

Tammy was taken to the local jail. She was booked with home invasion and having consensual sex with a minor. Steve and I were stunned and unable to process everything that had happened. I was seething and I didn't even visit her for the first month she was in jail.

We had our hands full trying to figure out what to do with the grandchildren to protect them. I knew I had to force myself to move beyond my own feelings to be able to help everyone in the family, but it was a struggle.

Tammy's fourteen year old son, Stephen Ray, came to live with Steve and I. Tammy's two other girls, Amber and Morgan, were with their father and other grandparents. Tammy's younger daughter, Cheyenne, went to live with Stephanie and her husband Chad.

Stephanie was livid with Tammy because of what she was putting the family through, and because she had violated the trust of her children. Once again she felt she had no choice, but to pick up the pieces of Tammy's addiction.

I had to admire Stephanie - she had guts and she had courage - but she had a long road ahead before she could forgive Tammy. She knew that she had to find a way to forgiveness for the sake of Cheyenne. We all began to realize forgiveness is sometimes a process.

House of Heartbreak

Tammy was in the county jail, alone and frightened. When I moved past my anger, I went to visit her. She came to the window; she looked like death warmed over; her hands were shaking uncontrollably. She cried and cried. My heart was broken for her, the kids, and for all of us.

Oh, God, how did we get to this awful place? I trusted God was in charge, but I couldn't make sense of any of this. I was praying for answers. What had happened to this child of mine? How did her life stray onto this path? The Tammy I knew loved children, and would never bring harm to any one of them. Getting high was no excuse for what she had done.

At this point I had no answers. I was in shock and disbelief. Overnight, Steve and I were required to alter our perceptions; our world had been turned upside down. Both of us were experiencing feelings of unreality and helplessness. We were having a hard time concentrating, were losing things, and found it hard to make decisions. We hoped those feelings would pass quickly.

In jail, Tammy was dealing with her own set of problems. She had no choice but to settle into the routine. Generally, people are in county jail a day or two, or at the most, a couple of weeks. County jail is a hard place to be for a long term, because it isn't setup for prolonged incarceration.

Beds were temporary. People came in and out through a revolving door. Tammy had to buy all of her own toiletries, and then struggled to keep them from being stolen. Some of the inmates were plain mean, seasoned hard criminals; most were scared. Families had to check in and wait a long time before they could visit the inmates. If they did not abide by every single rule, they were thrown out.

I felt my heartbreaking when I saw the children visiting. It was pitiful to watch their sadness when leaving their mother or father. The children couldn't understand why their parent was in jail; why they had to be quiet, and why they couldn't touch their parent. The parents were sorry at that point, but it was far too late for them to help their children.

In my opinion, our new female district attorney wanted to make a name for herself. She told everyone she'd make an example of Tammy. She was pushing for the maximum sentence, and was ruthless in her dealings with Tammy.

Emotionally, shame and guilt were eating Tammy up. She was going through drug withdrawal, and believe me, there is no soft cushion for it in prison. Steve and I decided we were going to let the public defender represent her. We were financially tapped out and we were determined that we would not pick up the pieces any more.

Tammy was sentenced to seven years in the state penitentiary after seven months in county jail. Steve and I, and the children were heartbroken; tears and sadness being our new friends. Life had to go on.

I settled into routinely visiting Tammy in the state penitentiary once a week. Occasionally, I would take Stephen and Cheyenne with me. I began to see changes in Tammy. She was becoming the person I always knew she could be, no longer underneath all that addiction.

It was nice to see her clear headed with her hands no longer shaking. I was sad that most of my friends only knew Tammy as a drug addict. I was still asking the question "why?" Why did her life take the drug path?

Raymond, Tammy's first husband, started visiting her. They developed a true friendship. He encouraged her to hold her head up and move forward. Tammy was accepted into the drug rehab program and learned about the nature of addiction, including how to cope with it, and how not to relapse.

I took Tammy a journal and asked her to start writing daily about her experiences in prison. I knew she always liked to write; I figured it would give her something to do.

Tammy started writing and also drawing. The pictures were incredibly interesting, and I realized she must have gotten some of my artistic talent. Oddly, I didn't know that before. When I later read her journals, I appreciated her incredible snapshot of prison life.

She noted most of the inmates' time was spent trying not to get into conflict with the guards. Tammy got a job as a teacher's assistant to help other inmates learn to read. Many of the inmates were illiterate. That year Steve and I received the following Father's Day and Mother's Day poems from Tammy:

My Mother, My Mentor, My Friend

~Tammy Hoskins

The first memories I have are of 'Green Eggs and Ham',
And trailing you to the kitchen to lend you a hand.
Never once did you tell me no, you're not able.
You just pulled up a chair and handed the ladle.
Then as I grew with a young girl's insecurities
You gave me words of encouragement,
You said I was pretty.
When my young heart was aching, I cried rivers of tears,
You were always there to comfort me, and allay my fears.
When I broke your heart by the life I was living,
You buried your pain, and just kept on giving.
It was then that I realized that you're not just my mother,
You're the best friend I've had set above others.
If I had only one wish, I know what it would be,
To give you back all that you've given to me.
Not only that, there's one more part,
I'd give my very life to heal your heart!

Don't Ever Give Up

~ *Tammy Hoskins*

I said, look dad, no hands, with a little girl's pride,

On the bright sunny day that you taught me to ride.

But you and I know that I didn't get very far,

When I ran right into your shiny new car.

You didn't get angry. You didn't get tough.

You said try again, and don't ever give up.

Then there was a time that you taught me to drive,

You seemed so relaxed, at least on the outside.

When I grounded the gears you didn't think I saw,

You were working the clutch on your side of the car.

You didn't get angry. You didn't get tough.

You said, try again and don't give up.

Now life has gone on, and the road has been rough,

I've been through some changes, and some real ugly stuff,

But I paid attention dad, I've listened to you

And now I know what it is I must do.

So I'll try again dad, I won't ever give up

And I haven't said I love you near often enough.

Dad, have a wonderful Father's Day,

You've taught me so many things,

And although at the time it appeared I was not listening,

I was.

Thank you for being my dad.

I love you, Tammy.

The first day Tammy came to the visiting area in her prison clothes, I tried hard not to show how much it hurt to see her like that.

I noticed the guards were a mixed lot. Some of them treated people with respect and others abused their power. One day, while visiting Tammy, I watched two kids who came to see their mother. The kids were laughing while their mother was entertaining them. They weren't too loud, but the guard motioned them out the door.

The visit was terminated because the kids were laughing. The kids had only been there about ten minutes, and the family had driven over one hundred-fifty miles to see their mom. The kids cried as they were escorted out the door.

Later, I heard that the guard, who had made the kids leave, was reprimanded for being offensive toward a different family. She was downright mean. (I guess she picked the wrong family to offend.) Laughing under my breath; I thought she deserved more than a reprimand. I doubted being forced to take time off made a difference in her meanness. I always watched my P's and Q's, not wanting my visits terminated early.

Prison was a disheartening place, and visiting was a challenge in patience. Visitors were searched and treated like criminals. Visitation took a whole day as the wait could be two or three hours before being allowed in the holding area and then another hour long wait to get in the visiting area. The dark energy in the prison was palpable; stress and strong emotions oozed from the prisoners and visitors.

There was stress of not knowing how long a person could see a loved one, the stress of visiting under tightly controlled conditions, as well as the stress of eventually parting. I heard inmates ask desperately, "Will you still love me?" "Will you wait for me?"

Our prisons are full of people who are mentally ill and addicted in some way. Personally, I thought incarcerating the mentally ill and addicts was a terrible social solution. Many prisoners had lived hard lives on the outside; suffering sexual, physical and mental abuse. Prisoners trusted no one. Why should they? Often inmates were not trustworthy, either. They were masters at manipulation, a useful skill for survival.

Tammy was a lucky one. She had grown up with a family who always loved her. Many of the inmates had no one, couldn't read or write, and had no self-esteem. Their lives were at an all-time low with no way out of the black hole of prison. It broke my heart to see the children crying when it was time to leave their mother or father. Still even in prison, prisoners were manipulating and conniving. A part of me knew it took much pain to get in a place like that?

The Shadow of My Brain

~Sharron Magyar

You're hiding in the shadow of my brain,

Every moment cloaked with your presence.

I can't allow my thoughts to land there,

Too much sadness to bear.

You were my child, yet I knew you not at all,

Secret thoughts as vile as cancer eating away your smile.

You'll always be there in my heart, sadness tucked away.

Maybe one day I'll figure it all out.

What happened?

Raymond's Story

When Tammy went to prison, Raymond, her first husband and the father of my grandson, Stephen Ray, called to ask if he could see Stephen Ray. He had tried before, but Tammy and her new husband refused to let him see his son.

I hadn't seen Raymond in fourteen years. Both Tammy and Raymond had gone down the path of drug addiction. The telephone call went like this, "Sharron, I heard what happened with Tammy and I wanted to let you know I'm available to help with Stephen Ray."

I told him I appreciated his offer, but I had concerns about him being involved in Stephen Ray's life since I knew he was still drugging. We talked a while, and then I told him he had it within himself to quit doing drugs, and I would be willing to teach him self-hypnosis.

I hung up the phone thinking about Raymond. I remembered he was the type of kid who knew who was calling before the phone even rang. I could never surprise him with gifts when he was married to Tammy. He could always tell me what they were before he opened them. I wondered if his drug abuse took his giftedness underground.

Raymond called a week later. He said, "I've been thinking about what you said to me about my being able to get off the drugs, and I'm willing to try." He also told me about a vision he'd had. "I saw you and me on the Oprah Winfrey Show, and we were talking about the book that you had written about my life. The book was to help children not go down the drug path I took."

It was an interesting idea, although I couldn't possibly envision the two of us doing a book together. I was organized and time conscious. Raymond didn't have a sense of time, or know how to be organized. I also knew a project of that scope would take a lot of time. I imagined him always being an hour late, with me waiting and wanting to wring his neck.

Besides all that, I had just taken on raising a grandchild, and had Tammy in prison. I was just plain tired from recently graduating from college. I couldn't imagine having the energy to think about a project of that size.

A few days later, my youngest sister, Nancy, called and asked me what I'd been up to. There's eleven years between us, and I absolutely adore her. Nancy put herself through school to get a Doctorate in Psychology. She is logical, analytical, and has a great personality.

She has been the one person who helped Tammy in any way she could. I could always count on her to listen to what I was struggling with in respect to Tammy. She had a cool head and gave me great advice.

Nancy called me one day and as we were chatting I told her what Raymond had said about doing a book together. Nancy cut me off with, "Wait a minute. Wait a minute. I see the book. It's brightly colored like your artwork, and the images are mosaic-like. I see you and Raymond sitting on the floor, and he's telling you his story while he's in a trance."

For thirty minutes, information rolled out of her mouth about the book. I hung up the phone. My head was reeling with all the stuff she'd said. You have to understand, Nancy is one of the most grounded people I know. The whole conversation took me by surprise.

I began to think about the book more, but ultimately stayed in the same place - resistance! I was too tired to take on a project of that size. I couldn't imagine how long it might take to do a book. The time issue hadn't gone away for me. Yet, the book idea nagged at me. One reason I was so committed to going to school at Washington University was because I felt it was supposed to help me with books I was supposed to write. This wasn't exactly the book I had envisioned. I thought I would be writing a fairy book for children in order to help them deal with physical pain. God had bigger plans for me.

A week later my friend, Diane, came over. Diane is a friend everyone should have. She had a peculiar way of showing up when I needed a friend the most. She carefully listened to what I had to say, never judged, and was funny and quirky. She made me laugh no matter how difficult life was for me. She had a high degree of intuition that she just accepted, assuming everyone had her special gift.

That particular day she said, "I'm going to tell you something that doesn't make any sense to me at all, but I know I'm supposed to give you this message. I was sitting at the pizza place at K-Mart eating lunch, minding my own business, when all of a sudden I had a vision. (Seemed like those days everyone was having visions.) You were sitting on the edge of a pier, and it was like you were about to jump off. I am also supposed to tell you it won't take any longer than it took you to drive back and forth to St. Louis to school. Do you know what this means?"

I started laughing. Yes, I knew what it meant. I told her about the book that Raymond and Nancy had envisioned and about my resistance. I was still resisting. However, everyone else had visions of it happening around me.

Another week went by. I got an email from Cheryl Lynn, my lifelong friend from in Las Vegas who was very familiar with my struggles. We often spent time on the phone talking about our children and comparing notes. She had encouraged me to go to school, assuring me that I could do it. The email went like this, "I don't know what you're resisting, but you are supposed to do it." Okay, so I get it. I guess I will be writing a book with Raymond.

My orientation was that the book was an art project. Raymond and I began to consider the idea. From what my sister Nancy and Raymond had told me, the book was to be the story of Raymond's life, which he would talk though while in a trance.

We came to the conclusion that we would do just that. We talked and talked and talked about the implications of doing the book. Both Raymond and I stayed very much committed to the idea. We thought it could help abused children.

First Session: We went to the park, sat on a blanket, and began. I had my painting materials at my side. I talked to Raymond in a very soothing voice, and soon he dropped into a trance. He started by recounting life with his mother when he was four years old. He loved his mother with all his heart. I started recording his story in drawings and we moved forward.

Second Session: Raymond went back to the incident when he saw his mother being run over by a train. Christmas came and Raymond didn't know why his mother wasn't there. He asked God to bring her home. He promised to be good. His older brother, Frank, took him out and bought him a toy gun for Christmas. He explained to Raymond his mother was never coming back. Raymond believed it was entirely his fault she was gone; he pleaded with God to bring her home. He would be good.

Raymond's life had irrevocably changed at five years old. Not until he was forty-five years old and not until his work with shamanism and hypnosis is he able to heal the wounds that drove his life. Abandonment had been his life's sentence.

Raymond's Comments:

I have lived most of my life in fear. Until recently, I couldn't forgive my mom for leaving me at five years old, and for making me live the life that I have lived. It took me forty-two years to get over the belief that my mom had not left me on purpose. Reality was, the loss of Mom didn't make me make bad decisions, I did.

Sometimes fear makes a person stronger. It makes a person want to get things done in their life. Then there are people like me. Fear overtakes them so much that they're afraid to step out of it because that's not their reality.

Their reality is to live in a box of fear and stay hidden away from everybody. Do a little crime here and there, and then go hide - almost like a little groundhog. Hey, I'm going to go out and see the neighbors, and run back in fast. That's what fear did for me.

Small things started linking together for me each day as I started working with hypnosis. As I put in each link, the chain got stronger. I learned everything didn't have to be black and white for me. I kept blowing things up big. I started learning about the psychic abilities that I have. I finally began to realize that little things really did matter.

When I started using my abilities to help people, my life started turning around. It was about me reaching out and trying to help other children not take the path that I had taken. That is when I decided to let all the innards go. I wanted to help other kids, the ones that are like I was - frozen in fear.

Raymond's Interview:

I asked, "How do you find it within yourself to forgive yourself and God?"

Raymond's answered, *"I was angry with God for taking my mother. It was a bad time in my life, but I realized I wanted to go to the same place with her, so I had to forgive God to do that. Most importantly, I had to be able to forgive myself first, for saying bad things about God. I could forgive everyone else, but I couldn't forgive myself for what I had done to myself."*

I asked, "Forgiving yourself was the hardest thing you ever did?"

Raymond's answered, *"No, forgiving me was the ability to love myself; and that was the hardest thing that I ever did."*

I asked, "Why was it so hard to love yourself?"

Raymond's answered: *I couldn't love myself because I had so much hatred for everything around me. The person, who could show me the most love, was taken from me at five. At seven, the next people that I thought could love me molested me. I didn't know what love was. In my world, love meant you conquer and hurt. When I tried to tell someone about what was happening, I was thrown to the wolves. That's why I was so violent when I was growing up, and always in trouble. I had to be in control, and that meant I had to hurt people to get them to love me. I just found out a few years ago that that's not true.*

Now I take life every day, every second, as it is. I don't plan things ahead. I don't worry about yesterday, because I can't bring it back and I can't change it. I don't worry about whether tomorrow is going to come or not.

I've got to live for who I am right now, today at this moment. I have learned to love myself and learned to care for things. Most importantly, I care about the people around me. That's what makes me who I am now and why I put my heart out to help people today.

Closure

Many times we go through life having a traumatic experience like Raymond did and we relive the event in our minds over and over. What keeps us stuck? Why can't we move forward in our hearts and our thoughts? Sometimes the answer is in finding closure.

Has your mind ever gone to: "Why me? Why was someone mean to me? Why couldn't they love me? Why couldn't I stop thinking about them?" What do you really need from the person or situation, to bring closure to your heart? Realistically, other people cannot provide you with what you need for closure, but identifying the need can open the door toward forgiveness, and letting go.

Create a ritual that is meaningful to you or use the following visualization. Using imagery in hypnosis can be a rapid way of creating closure. What is created in our mind has the power to heal the heart.

Soul Exercise 16: Forgiveness

The following meditation utilizes a cord cutting technique. Among healers, the sharing of energy between people is referred to as cording. The cord signifies energetic tubing connecting two individuals together. People that energetically exchange or give away energy in their relationship generally end up with one person becoming powerless while the other person gets stronger. The inappropriate chording makes the weakened person feel energetically and emotionally overpowered because of giving away his/her soul energy, while the strengthened person craves more and more of the joint energy.

- ♥ Take a deep breath. Breathe deeply into your belly for seven counts; hold your breath for seven counts; exhale for seven counts, and hold for seven counts. Repeat this process seven times. Focus on releasing all the negativity while exhaling. Breathe in tranquility and peace as you inhale. Breathe out stress and tension as you exhale. Eventually, you will step into a natural breathing rhythm and fall into a deep relaxation.

- 💗 When you are completely relaxed, visualize a rose garden in your mind. Imagine you are winding down the path to the center where there is a bench. The space in the garden is protected. You are safe.

- 💗 Imagine the person you would like to bring closure with waiting for you at the center. When you arrive at the bench make eye contact with the other person.

- 💗 *Tell the person what you are still angry about. . . . Listen to their reply.*

- 💗 *Tell the person what you feel they owe you. . . . Listen to their reply, and then tell them what you owe them.*

- 💗 *Tell the person what you need to forgive them for. . . . Listen to their reply.*

- 💗 *Tell the person what you learned from them.*

- 💗 *Tell the person what you wish for them.*

- 💗 *Ask yourself what you need to forgive yourself for.*

- 💗 *Visualize a cord going from the person to yourself and cut the cord. Send a white energetic light down the cord to the other person to provide healing for them. . . . . Let go of your stuck feelings and expand your heart.*

- 💗 Count yourself up to five and bring your awareness back in to the room.

The weak can never forgive. Forgiveness is the attribute of the strong.

~Mahatma Gandhi

8

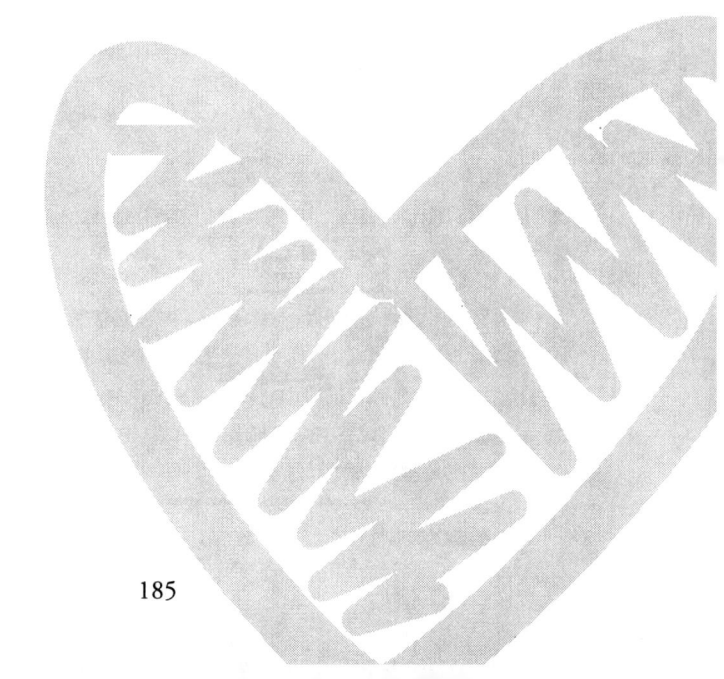

Trauma

The body has efficient mechanisms to cope with stress. One being dissociation, a defense method that can help people tolerate or minimize stress. It is also a form of self-hypnosis which everyone experiences occasionally. Other examples of dissociation are day-dreaming, fantasizing and spacing out.

There are varying levels of dissociation.

When a child or person experiences trauma they will use a stronger form of dissociation wherein they will experience a sense that the "self" or world is unreal. They can also experience loss of memory by either completely forgetting personal identity, or fragmentation of identity. Traumatic dissociation is linked with the following responses:

- Numbness of general responsiveness.
- Deadened emotions.
- Leaving one's body.
- Withdrawal.
- Re-experiencing trauma.

These symptoms can result in sleep disturbances, concentration and memory problems, as well as anxiety and depression.

Often the individual cannot remember the original wounding event, yet they may experience extreme emotions of numbness, guilt, anger, avoidance, sadness, hopelessness, helplessness, negative self-evaluation and shame. All of these emotions can negatively influence personal relationships.

Compounding the problem, those feelings are often accompanied by hyper-awareness & intensification of symptoms.

In instances of acute trauma, dissociation helps an individual see the mind and body as separate from the wound. The body creates a condition to physically distance the real identity. It can seem as if the person is the observer watching a movie.

When I was walking across a street and hit by a car, it was if I could see in my mind myself getting hit, and it felt as if it was happening in slow motion. When a person experiences dissociation, distortion of the size and shape of things can feel surreal.

A traumatized person can feel as if they are disconnected from the body, or floating outside of it, and traveling to another location. Sensory perceptions may seem distorted such as the world seems intensely colored or colorless. Sounds may seem extremely loud or silent. Distorted feelings can last for a few moments or for years.

The function of the dissociation to trauma is to spare the person from being overwhelmed by imagining that the traumatic event is not happening, or it can operate as an escape from physical and emotional pain.

If the trauma is severe and prolonged, partially or fully formed identities with specific roles may be created. These personalities often control a person's behavior. They may be accompanied by memory loss not explained by ordinary forgetfulness. Fully formed identities can give the impression that different people are talking in a person's head.

The second way the mind and body deal with trauma is by encapsulating the energy of trauma, and imprinting it in the body and subconscious mind. When a person experiences a trauma, the limbic-hypothalamic system programs the emotional state of fear into the body and subconscious. This programming provides protection from what an individual recognizes as danger, and prepares the body for fight or flight.

Trauma may not always be in your conscious awareness. Birth trauma and past life trauma remain in the subconscious mind, yet often without any conscious memory of the wounds. All shocking events leave wounds in the subconscious influencing the person's present.

If trauma constantly repeats itself, a pattern may gradually develop that causes an ever-increasing split in the soul. Traumas may be carried far into the future if they are not healed. Soul wounds from traumas can cause an individual to become immobilized with soul fragmentation and energetic soul loss.

Releasing an encapsulated soul wound can be accomplished in various ways. Focused attention, imagery, biofeedback, massage, acupuncture, and sound therapy can release wounds. In my opinion, the most efficient and least stressful ways of releasing a wound are through hypnosis or breathwork.

The ability to connect "without the concept of time" allows the release of trauma, making changes in belief systems fast and lasting. Using hypnosis or breathwork allows healing to be accepted by the subconscious as real.

One way to check for energetic soul loss is by examining a person's feelings. A person with soul loss feels empty, lost, and un-whole. Occasionally, they feel they are being controlled by someone else.

Another way to verify soul loss is to ask a shaman to energetically inspect the soul. They may see fragmentation, missing parts, holes, blotches or a tunnel through the soul. The shaman can also visually inspect the soul to see if threads or cords are coming out of the soul. Cords or fragments can be traced to the missing soul parts, either inside or outside the body. These cords may also be attached to another person.

Recently, I accompanied my husband, who suffers from post-traumatic stress syndrome to the veteran's clinic. As an Army medic in Vietnam, he saw a lot of trauma and death. While we were at the clinic, Steve's doctor started a conversation about post traumatic stress disorder.

She commented, "I do surgery all the time and see traumatic things; I just make up my mind to forget it. You can do that, just make up your mind to forget it." I was steaming when I heard those words coming out of the VA doctor's mouth. There was an element of judgment, implying that because she does not experience PTSD and Steve does, that he could just think it away.

I went home and thought about what it was that the doctor wasn't getting about PTSD. What was the difference between her doing surgery involving trauma, that did not cause a problem for her, and the surgery that my husband performed in the field as a Viet Naum soldier which left him with PTSD?

One difference being, Steve was exposed to a traumatic situation in the field, with not only his own life in danger, but those of the soldiers he was working on. When his life was threatened, an "out of time" state was created, which presented an opportunity for wounds to be recorded on my husband's soul and body.

I think my husband has a very good doctor, but in this one respect I believe she needed more understanding.

It takes a considerable amount of daily energy to maintain soul wounds; as they divert energy from physical and emotional processing. A soul wound that involves physical trauma or impact can cause energy leaks, blocks, and imprints.

This then promotes dysfunction and disease in the body. Any trauma that is severe enough to occur in an "out-of-time" state can create a situation in which a person can become frozen in fear.

The mind and body are beautiful and ingenious. They can encapsulate the energy of soul wounds and suspend them in the body to be healed at a future date. Its resourcefulness can be accessed to heal a soul wound painlessly in an instant, given the proper environment and circumstances.

Shamanism

Shamanic methods have been documented to be at least twenty thousand years old, and have been used over hundreds of generations. Their orientation is to promote health and utilize the healing potential of the mind. Shaman's journey back and forth between our current reality and an altered state which they may enter through prayer, chanting, drumming dancing or other ceremonial rituals.

Once the shaman enters the altered state, he can contact spirit guides, angels and other shamans to receive wisdom and advice for performing healing tasks. The shaman seeks deeper truths, as well as insight for understanding and healing.

A shaman's job is often to look for missing soul parts. These parts may be found inside or outside the body. If found inside the body, they are encapsulated by energy and held until the individual chooses to access the event that caused soul loss. A person can often see their soul parts and retrieve them themselves while in a trance state.

If the soul part is outside the body, it may be necessary to retrieve it by way of an intervention. In more difficult situations, a soul part may also be possessed by an attaching earthbound entity, the soul of a living person, or a dark entity. In this situation, it is better to leave soul retrieval to a qualified shaman trained in soul retrieval.

From an early age a shaman is taught the importance of the intact soul, knowing that any lost or stolen parts should be retrieved to maintain emotional, mental and physical health. Shamanism offers an ideal way to return to past trauma because it incorporates a trance state which is emotionally or physically nonthreatening.

With shamanism, most people can achieve in a few hours what might otherwise have taken years to heal. Specific techniques long used in shamanism utilize changes in state of consciousness, visualization, and positive thinking.

As a society, we are accustomed to relying on an outside source such as drugs to provide solutions to our problems. I agree there is a case for the use of medically prescribed drugs, but have concerns about their overuse. Today, prescription drug use is at epidemic proportions. Unfortunately our health is being compromised through our easy and free access to prescription drugs.

Progressively-minded people are willing to explore other avenues using alternative modalities to support wellness and health.

Shamanism, as well as hypnosis, can promote positive transformation without inflicting further trauma. By exploring soul loss in a trance state, the soul can be recalled, discharged, and understood. The split or lost soul part can be cleansed, healed, and filled with light for reintegration.

Calling on angels to help can also be beneficial. The beauty in using a trance state is that your subconscious releases events and emotions centered around the trauma, so that you are permanently healed, gently and easily.

As always, be sure to do your due diligence before working with a shaman or a hypnotist. Check their credentials, education and experience.

Jason

I met Jason at the National Guild of Hypnotists Convention in Boston. After presenting our classes, a group of us went out to dinner. We were excited about exchanging and sharing new ideas about hypnosis. As I got to know Jason better, he told me he'd been in a head-on car collision five years ago. Both he and his daughter were critically injured. Since the accident, he had not been able to recover his energy which made him need a lot of sleep.

However, when he tried, he was unable to go to sleep. Along with sleep deprivation, he had continual debilitating migraine headaches. Although the doctors could not find anything wrong, he said he knew that he was just not the same since the accident. This made my ears perk up. We talked further, and agreed to do a session to look at his problem under hypnosis.

My intention was to combine shamanism and hypnosis to explore his problem. After calling forth protective energy to surround us, we began. Because Jason was a consulting hypnotist, he didn't need much prompting to get into a relaxed state.

Knowing there are seven main energy centers (chakras) in the body, I asked Jason to look at his chakras and tell me what he saw. He didn't notice anything out of the ordinary. Sometimes under hypnosis people can notice an abnormal condition in their own chakras.

They may be out of balance, turning the wrong direction, having blocked energy, or be turned inside out. Physical distress, migraines, and panic attacks can be the result of dysfunction in the chakras. I was searching to see what was happening to his energy.

Next, I asked Jason if he could imagine stepping out of his body, and look at it as if he were an observer. Because he was experienced in hypnosis, I thought he would be capable of performing this Shamanic technique and he was. I then directed him to go back in time to the beginning of the car accident and observe it in slow motion.

He started right before the car impact. Upon impact, he told me he could see his energy shoot out of his inner eye in anger toward the woman that had hit him. His inner eye was stuck in an open position, with energy flowing out of it. In his flight or fight response, he instinctually sent out protection for his daughter.

With horror, he realized his energy had been flowing out of his inner eye and directed in anger at the woman ever since the accident. Understanding began to flood his consciousness. I asked him if he was ready to bring his energy back to himself, and what conditions would he need to meet fulfill that. He said he knew he needed to forgive the woman for hitting them. (Note: I did not know what the conditions were, he did.)

Jason was contrite, and afraid that he had in some way hurt the woman who had hit them. I explained to Jason that his anger was elicited as a fight or flight response; he was not responding out of malicious intent. The loss of energy was hurting him more than anyone.

I guided Jason to step back into his body and draw the energy back into his body through his third eye. He drew his energy back into his body and it filled his body, then surrounded and radiated far outside his body. We ended the session with positive suggestions about his headaches, energy and health.

Jason's experience is a perfect example of an energetic response "out of conscious awareness." He had no idea he had the anger. It was concealed in his subconscious, yet that anger had serious repercussions for him.

Frozen Anger

Jason's life was being held hostage because he was frozen in anger (although it was out of his conscious awareness). The consequence of projecting his anger was low energy and ongoing migraine headaches.

Generally, anger develops because of what someone else has done to you, and often the response is distorted by the perceived hurt. The key to dissolving anger is forgiveness. Sometimes, we get so stuck in our anger that we think to ourselves, "I'll never forgive them". The inability to forgive renders us the victim and makes us powerless.

It's so easy to stay angry by telling yourself, "They ruined my life; they did it on purpose; I was little and they hurt me so much." Unresolved anger stuck in the subconscious plants seeds for disease in the body. Anger causes a loss of your inner monitoring ability, and in unbiased observability.

Feelings of anger are neither good nor bad. When you have been mistreated or wronged it is healthy and normal to feel angry. Angry feelings are not the problem—it is the choices you make in response to the anger that often can be a problem.

Ghosts

~Sharron Magyar

I had them stacked in my closet;
They are all the people I cannot forgive.
They've hurt me, lied and cheated again and again.
I could spend all day in my room and never be alone,
For all I have to do is think of my ghosts,
And I am angry all over again.
They whisper, laugh and mock me,
I cannot open the door for they will only bring pain
I fear, I have to leave it shut in my trembling and rage,
I know I can treat others just the way they treated me.
Make a ghost out of them, quickly they disappear.
But then I find I'm behind the door of my own pain.
A ghost lost with the rest, begging for release.
My spirit just a ghost, locked out of reality.

Soul Exercise 17: Healing Anger

Always do meditation in a relaxing, private place. You may tape record this meditation and play it back.

- ♥ *Focus your eyes on a spot on the ceiling. Stare at it until the muscles around your eyes become tired. Take a deep breath. Breathe deeply into your belly for seven counts; hold your breath for seven counts; exhale for seven counts, and hold for seven counts. Repeat this process seven times. Focus on releasing all the negativity while exhaling. Breathe in tranquility and peace as you inhale. Breathe out stress and tension as you exhale. Eventually, you will step into a natural breathing rhythm and fall into a deep relaxation. Imagine that you are breathing stress out of your toes. Breathe, and feel the air against your nostrils.*

- ♥ *Let your breath go deeply into your lungs while expanding them. Hold, and then breathe out. Imagine in your mind that you are at the top of the staircase .... There are 20 steps going down .... Start at the number 20 stepping down; as you step down, relax the body .... 19 Relaxing more ... 18 Letting go of stress . ... 17 Calm and relaxed .... 16 Releasing conflict .... 15 Calm and relaxed ..... 14 Smooth and easy .... 13 Deeper and deeper .... 12 Relaxing the mind .... 11 relaxing the body .... 10 More relaxed .... 9 Relaxed . ... 8 Going down .... 7 More calm .... 6 Doubling your relaxation .... 5 .... Whatever doubling might be for you .... 4 .... 3 .... 2 ..... 1.*

- ♥ *Step out into a hallway which has many doors. Walk down the hallway and find the room labeled* "anger". Give yourself permission to enter into this room. In this room you will see things that symbolize what you're angry at . . . . Some things you're aware of. Others will surprise you . . . . Observe carefully what the room contains.

- 💗 Pick out the most important issue or person you are drawn to at this time, and understand the anger connection.

- 💗 Now imagine that you are standing right in front of yourself as your wisest self . . . . As a wise person, give yourself advice about how to deal with this anger.

- 💗 Give your anger a picture that represents it . . . . What color is it? How is it shaped? How does it smell? How does it sound? Can you give yourself permission to either destroy the picture, or transform it into something more positive? Make the changes that intuitively seem right for you.

- 💗 Ask yourself if the process is complete for you. Is there anything else that you need to do in this room? If the answer is yes, do it now. When you are ready - come out of the anger room, and close the door behind you. Or you may choose to burn down the anger room all at once.

- 💗 Count from one to five, bringing your awareness back into the room. Feel love entering your body as you put your feet on the ground and stretch. (You may find that you have to visit the anger room many times, if you are holding a lot of anger or you may choose to deal with it all at once.) If you are revisiting the room, be persistent until all the anger has dissolved.

Smacked Out Of Time

In 2006, I went to my sister's in Indiana to help her pack and move. I was packing in the basement and it was a little dark, so I decided to go to Goodwill to buy a lamp. When I got there the store wasn't open yet. I parked my car and walked across the street to McDonald's to get a cup of coffee and wait.

At ten o'clock, I started to walk back across the street to the Goodwill store. The street was clear both left and right as I started to cross it. Something made me turn around and look behind me. Suddenly, I realized there was a car behind me pulling out of McDonalds and I knew the car was going to hit me!

Time stood still.

It was as if I was moving in slow motion. I tried to get out of the way, but the car smacked into my back right hip. The impact was so forceful it slammed me down on the asphalt, and I passed out. When I regained consciousness, I was looking up at the underside of the car. For a moment I was numb, and then feeling began to enter my body. The pain was excruciating.

The driver, a mother with a crying baby in the backseat, had turned around to see what was wrong with her baby. She didn't see me until she hit me.

Next thing I knew the police and ambulance arrived to take me to the hospital. The police took the driver's information. She lied saying she had insurance. It was my unlucky day, she didn't have insurance.

Getting hit by the car changed my life permanently and in many ways. Before I was hit, I had excellent hand-eye coordination and memory, was well organized and could prioritize. I could right away spell any word I heard and read ten to twelve books a week. I was physically active and involved in sports.

After the accident, I was instantly ADHD. I could no longer read and spell, and would transpose numbers and letters. My ability to organize was gone; I had problems staying on task, and I could not remember things.

Many of my physical abilities were compromised, also. I had no sense of balance and fell easily; I could no longer engage in any sport; I was constantly in excruciating pain, and walking anywhere was impossible for me. I had no broken bones, so to look at me you couldn't tell that anything was wrong. I knew plenty was wrong.

Of course, the first thing I did was to try to get help from my doctor. He wanted to put me on painkillers which didn't seem like a good solution for me. In addition, I went to a chiropractor for a year, but had no way to evaluate whether he was helping me or not, because I was in so much pain.

I knew that humans are hardwired to heal because of my granddaughter Morgan's experience, and I was determined that I was going to find ways to heal myself. I began to use hypnosis to visualize and remember what healthy meant for me. I put out the intention that the Universe would bring me the right people to help me with my healing. The door opened with many people walking into my life.

I first began doing work with Brain Gym movements (http://braingym.org/about) "Brain Gym® movements, exercises, or activities refer to the original 26 Brain Gym movements, sometimes abbreviated as the 26. These activities recall the movements naturally done during the first years of life while learning mind/body co-ordination.

The Brain Gym practitioner I worked with gave me the task of practicing cross crawls, jumping jacks, figure eights with eye movements, and an assortment of other physical exercises.

It was difficult for me to do a simple cross crawl. I practiced the movements over and over, so my mind and body could reconnect with movement memories. When I had mastered some of the movements, some of my coordination came back, a little more balance, and my thinking was slightly clearer. At least I could now walk without holding onto things.

Kinesiology

I decided to get my certification in Brain Gym. I knew my instructor's work had been beneficial for children suffering from ADHD, and that she was respected by other healthcare practitioners. At the start of class, our instructor dragged eight long round cardboard tubes out of the closet. She told us we were going to do an experiential exercise.

We were to lie flat on the floor, and put the cardboard tubes under our backs. She then demonstrated how to roll the tubes up and down our spine. I wrestled the tube into place, rolled my back down it once, and then started back up. To my dismay, I started shaking like a leaf, and was immediately nauseated. I yelled to my partner to get the trash can so I could throw up in it. My body was reeling in shock.

Right away, I knew I had connected to the shock of getting hit by the car. Wave after wave of emotion was flooding my body. I was shaking from head to toe. I held on to the corner of the door steadying myself, so I wouldn't fall over.

Clay, my class partner was torn; he didn't know if he should hold onto me, or go get the trash can. Our instructor asked the students to come help me up and onto a massage table. My legs were shaky and weak. I was nauseated and I could barely stand up or breathe. She explained to the other students that I had pressed a release point where the trauma from the accident had been embedded in my body.

All the shock of getting hit by the car was coming to the surface. My instructor and the students did a series of Touch for Health checks and movements to balance my body.

According to the book *Touch for Health, a Practical Guide to Natural Health with Acupressure Touch*, "Touch for Health links certain muscles with specific organ systems - including the vascular and lymph system - and acupuncture meridians. When a particular muscle gets balanced, it may benefit the related organ or system. Monitoring the muscle response as an indication of energy flow and balance is the basis of TFH work." (Pg. 7)

I began to feel more centered and balanced after the students helped me with the movements. The nausea subsided as well as the shaking. I was still trying to wrap my head around what had happened.

The next day, I realized that ever since the accident, I had never felt safe in my body and I had a continual urge to look over my shoulder. What a lesson in the power of the subconscious mind. The shock of getting hit had literally become embedded in the body.

Some lessons really hit you hard. I got it!

Sound Therapy

The Universe kept sending me the right people at the right time to help on my healing journey. I gave up questioning and let it happen. I started sensing that my next step in healing was to use sound therapy, which employs the use of rhythmic sounds to discharge stress in the body.

In the book, *The Effects of Noise on Man*, Karl Kryter notes, "The effectiveness of morphine in the relief of postoperative pain is statistically about the same as the apparent effectiveness of audio analgesia in clinical dentistry." (Pg. 449) I was impressed. If sound could help with dental pain, then I generalized it could help with the pain I was experiencing from getting hit. I began more investigation into the healing use of sound.

In simple language, I discovered that high frequency sounds transmitted to the ear or other pressure points in the body release energy from the cortex of the brain. Rhythm frequencies of sound represent an energy that can influence the body frequencies. Sound can resynchronize our body rhythms. The theory resonated with me and I wondered where I might find a good sound therapist.

Within a week of deciding I needed to do sound therapy, I met a woman named Teri Freesmeyer. Teri's background is in Shamanism, Metaphysics, and Energy Medicine. I asked her if she did sound therapy. She laughed and said, "That's too funny, yes, and I've been getting guided to work with it more and more. " So we began a journey together.

In my third sound therapy session, Teri asked me what my goals were that day. I told her I still could not read. After getting hit by the car, I could read for about five minutes before my brain would shut off; a feeling very difficult to explain.

Books had always been an important part of my life, and I missed them terribly. When I wanted to learn anything, I always turned to books. I have to laugh, because more than once a book literally has fallen off the shelf and into my lap at the bookstore. It is a very expensive place for me to visit.

Teri was a gifted person who could easily connect with the higher realms for help. She tuned in and said she felt the work we needed to do that day was with the pineal gland. Lying on the massage table with my eyes closed, I relaxed and opened to the experience of sound.

Teri chose the didgeridoo playing deep earth sounds which rolled over my body. The sounds felt good. I began to daydream about a meadow. I smelled earth and grass. Next, she played the drums and I felt the pounding rhythm - solid, firm and insistent with waves entering my solar plexus.

My body then began to pulse in response to the drum music, and I drifted into another place when the drumming stopped.

I lost track of all time. Teri then picked up tuning forks and she softly hit different forks to set them in a vibration. She put each fork close to my ears. They were strange; some I heard more than others. The vibrations were persistent, and I felt some sort of shift in my hearing.

After what seemed a long while, she stopped playing the tuning forks, and picked up small bells to play. As she finished, she rang a final bell to call me back to ordinary reality.

I sat up and started to step down from the table when realized I was a little woozy. Something must have taken place. Only time would tell.

Two weeks passed when I called Teri to say, "Oh my gosh, Teri, I'm reading again. It's not perfect but it works for me. You have given me the gift of my heart's desire. Thank you."

Trust

At some point along the way, I began to realize I was grieving the loss of myself as I was before the accident. We think of grief when we have lost a loved one, nonetheless, we don't often recognize the ramifications of grief when we experience other personal losses.

I had clear memory of what I lost when I was hit by the car, yet I had no way of retrieving it. I had lost my ability to live a pain free life. The first several months I was in shock, literally numb in my body and emotions. Next, the pain set in - unbelievable and excruciating. I now understood how some people get addicted to drugs. They can be seductive, luring a person to numb the pain.

When the next issue surfaced, I saw myself mired in, "Why me? Why did I have to be hit? Why was someone so stupid they would be driving without insurance?" I found myself bargaining with God, "Please just turn back the clock and give me back myself". It is always easy to bargain with Him, when things aren't going well.

I was so angry with the woman who hit me, particularly, because she wasn't taking good care of her baby, and was driving without insurance. But also because hitting me had damaged my body and changed my life. I suspected she went on her merry way untouched. (There I go assuming again.) Occasionally, I still struggle with that one.

Next, I dropped down into a dark period of depression and isolated myself. I didn't want to see anyone. It took a Herculean effort to participate in any social functions. Internalizing the true magnitude of my loss depressed me. I felt emptiness and despair.

Forcing myself again to accept that life goes on, I started to adjust to life without my memory, coordination, or balance and with every aspect of myself in pain. The physical pain began to lose its sharp edge; it was still there, but not as throbbing. My mind slowly started functioning again. How can I help myself? Who do I need to seek out for help?

My memory was a serious problem; one minute I could remember anything I wanted in complete and minute detail. That made me smart, funny and self-confident. The next minute, I couldn't remember people's names, appointments, what I read, or what people told me; and even parts of my childhood memories were lost.

I went to the memory clinic with fear in my throat, wondering if maybe I was getting Alzheimer's (my dad had it). No Alzheimer's, yet no answers to what could be causing the problem either. It could be the traumatic impact of the accident, or it could be depression.

It could be standing on my head too much, as far as they knew. I tried the antidepressant, the standard medical solution the doctor recommended, and my body said, "Are you crazy?" "Oops, just thought I'd try."

The list of ways I've tried to help myself is extensive. Eventually, I stumbled on the question, "What am I supposed to be learning through this experience?"

One is acceptance; no holding on to what was, but accepting what is. Just because I couldn't comprehend the meaning of my suffering didn't mean there wasn't any. Although I couldn't remember appointments, I could figure out another way to remember that worked such as putting it in my phone with a reminder.

If I couldn't remember what I read, I could underline what I wanted to remember. Or I could learn through other avenues, like listening to audios rather than reading.

Another lesson that came with memory loss was empathy for myself and other people we shame because of what they cannot do. Sometimes we act and say things out of ignorance.

School children are shamed every day because they can't remember. Does it improve their memory? No, it just makes them cry.

Today I went to Sam's Club to replace my Sam's identification card, because I couldn't remember where I'd put it. When I asked the woman for a new card, she said gruffly, "This is the 13th one," with a stern look on her face. I felt my face filling with shame because I couldn't remember where my card was.

My memory resurfaced enough to tell her I'd only replaced my card twice, and that she shouldn't make me feel like a criminal about it. She stepped back a second, recognized her rudeness and then said that they start at number ten and the picture on the new card would be better anyway. What a nice change in attitude.

Last week my husband got upset with me because I couldn't find my car keys. Shame cropped up again. Just imagine how shamed people are when they cannot remember because they are stressed, have Alzheimer's, or are dealing with illness that affects their memory. Thankfully, I was able to challenge the woman's attitude at Sam's Club and found my voice. This leads me to my next lesson.

The last lesson I can readily think of is . . . . I can't remember what it was. Oh yes, I don't have to apologize. If you're uncomfortable with my lack of memory, it's your problem, not mine. I am adjusting to a less than razor sharp memory, as I am gaining compassion and generosity instead. If I remember next time I will tell you what else I have learned.

A new revelation for me was that God must have intended for me to learn something from my memory loss, and if that was His will, I could handle this experience. I began to accept the reality of my situation. Given the pain and turmoil I've experienced, I could never return to me as I was before this tragedy. I have traded my old ways to be more compassionate and loving to myself and others.

When I realized I would find a way forward, doors began to open. Different people from various alternative modalities began to appear in my life. Each of these people had a different piece of the puzzle to offer my healing. With each experience came understanding and learning about the nature of healing and the pain of wounds to the soul.

Do I still have pain? Yes. Do I still have moments when I can't remember what I was going to do or someone's name? Yes, sometimes. Do I still have trouble walking and have to be careful about my balance? Yes, definitely. What is important is how I choose to respond to all those things in my life.

> What lies behind us and what lies before us are tiny matters compared to what lies within us.
>
> ~Ralph Waldo Emerson

9 Addiction

Coming Down

~Sharron Magyar

Emotions riding high one moment, soaring the next.
Anticipation and elation beginning to crest,
Dropping down into the darkest depths.
How did I get on this rollercoaster?
Fear I must embrace, freezing time in my heart,
Sadness coming along on the journey
For the thrill has passed,
The journey has ended,
Yet I keep chasing after the ride.
My heart and my throat nervous in anticipation as I wait,
For the next moment to be revealed, and I know my fate.

Lisa

Lisa came to Golden Heart Hypnosis with the goal of improving her life. She had been in rehab 12 times for crack addiction with no long term success. She was desperate to get off drugs and figured trying hypnosis couldn't hurt anything. Lisa continually got high on crack, then would go on a bender prostituting for drugs.

I know from the experience with my daughter that working with addiction is not black and white; there are so many elements that enter into the picture. That being said, I do believe there is potential for success using hypnosis for some issues accompanying drug addiction if the person is motivated and persistent. The following is a description of an important session in Lisa's recovery.

Lisa had been struggling inside a broken and abusive relationship with her husband, and was in the process of divorcing him. At the same time, he was addicted to heroin. Her relationship with him was addictive, just like other aspects of her life. She was having a terrible time letting him go, even though she knew it was the best thing for her and her children.

Session: I assisted Lisa into a deep trance. I took her to the library where her book of life was written, and asked her to locate her book, which she easily did. She then brought the book over and put it on a table, and opened it. The first thing written on the page was the word "acceptance". It was what she came to work on in this lifetime. She read on, and the book said, "Let him go." She read about her children and about her relationship with them. She also read about her life's purpose.

Lisa realized she truly did need to let go of the relationship with her husband. Using a shamanic technique I supported her in retrieving the part of her soul she had given to him. She could visualize a cord going from her body to his, with the cord wrapped around and around him. She gently removed it, and sent him the energy of love.

It then occurred to me that she could have other soul parts that she needed to recover. I asked her, at this point and time in her life, if she would be ready to call other soul parts back to her. She replied, "Yes." I explained that by her intention, she could recover all the soul pieces at once. I then asked her to set the intention and call all of her soul parts back. She did.

What she saw amazed her. Every person she'd ever had sex with had a piece of her soul. She cried when she saw her soul parts coming home to her. I asked if there was an agreement that she had to make in order to accept the soul parts. She told me she was to keep her boundaries firm and strong. She was never to give away pieces of herself again. Lisa said she could feel the energy coming home to her, and she felt complete.

Interview with Lisa:

My question: Why didn't rehab work for you?

Lisa: It never really got to the problem.

My question: How did hypnosis help?

Lisa: It didn't immediately cure me, but as I worked with hypnosis my falls weren't as hard. I began to be able to instantly make a correction, rather than going out and getting on a two week binge that ended up with my prostituting for drugs. I am so used to creating chaos in my life I think if I can stop creating chaos, my life will change dramatically.

My question: Can you ever see yourself drug free?

Lisa: I am drug free right now. I made it 24 hours. If I can do it 24 hours at a time, I don't know why I can't do it for the rest of my life.

My question: What kinds of internal changes happened when you worked with hypnosis?

Lisa: I learned how to relax on my own, that was a big one. It took a while; it didn't happen overnight. There were some things we talked about together that stuck in my head. For example, staying in the solution rather than staying in the problem.

My question: I know your work took a shamanic turn. How important has it been to you to connect with your ancestors, spirit guides and angels on the other side? How much did that play into your recovery?

Lisa: I think a lot. Just knowing I had people pulling for me, who loved me on the other side, has been helpful. You have an idea but when it rings true, that's a different story.

My question: If you were to give someone advice, someone who is where you were five years ago, what advice would you give them?

Lisa: The three things that are critical to my recovery: My relationship with God, staying around people who are working the AA program and my hypnosis with shamanic work. All three of those things have worked together."

My question: How would you describe the struggle just to stay clean?

Lisa: You do what you don't want to do. It's not about being fun, or the rush, or any of that. After a while it's just pure addiction. I don't enjoy myself. I don't enjoy ruining my life. I don't enjoy hurting other people. I can't help myself, it's not fun, and it stopped being fun ten years ago. I realize now that a lot of my behavior was because I was sexually abused when I was young. It's not an excuse, it is a reality, and it has been a hard road to heal the damage done to me and I am still working on it. I don't set out to be irresponsible, or to be a bad person, or make bad decisions; there is a pull that I have a hard time controlling. I don't think about the consequences until after the fact.

My question: What if anything specific has hypnosis helped you within the range of all that?

Lisa: It has helped to raise my self-esteem. I didn't have any self-worth before.

My question: Do you feel that was about revisiting your trauma and connecting with the other side?

Lisa: It was about finding out that my life has purpose. I have a purpose for my life and I didn't even think like that until I started working with hypnotherapy. I didn't think my life was more than just my addiction, that there were other things I had to do while I was here.

My question: So connecting with your soul's purpose has made the shift for you?

Lisa: Yes.

> I do not understand what I do, for I want to do, I do not. But what I hate to do.
>
> ~*Romans 7:15*

Judgment

Like Lisa, many people have suffered from childhood abuse that led them to acting out inappropriately when they feel they have to provide safety for themselves. At the core of the unhealthy behavior is an addictive thought system which often leads to compulsive behavior. Compulsive behavior can come in many guises such as addiction to drugs, food, alcohol, pornography, and abusive relationships, to name a few. There is an obvious attempt to avoid feelings of isolation and shame.

The addicts' past history proves to them that their very survival is dependent on their ability to analyze, judge, categorize, and defend themselves. They must be quick about it. They measure every person and situation by information from the past, rather than present facts.

A tremendous amount of energy is lost for people who continually have to be reactive and on guard all the time. Their motto is to attack anything that threatens them, and to grab all they can, because the world they come from is a world of lack.

Every time addicts analyze, judge, categorize or defend to provide personal protection, chances are good they are not experiencing love. The Bible tells us the secret to being protected. It says we have to have integrity and uprightness. *(Psalms 25:21)*

Through hypnosis people visualize a better world for themselves, so they feel safe and protected. Resources such as self-love and integrity come from within to produce enduring change.

Hidden Memories

I sat at my designated place at the table in prison and Tammy sat at her designated place across the table from me. I had been thinking constantly of Tammy over the many months I visited her in prison and I absolutely knew something had to have happened to my daughter to make her take the path she took in her early teens.

I asked her, "Would you consider letting me hypnotize you to see if we can get to what is underneath all this?" She agreed, "I think it's a good idea."

Being as careful as I could, so as not to impose preconceived ideas on her and explaining to her she could raise her finger as a response to my questions, I began talking to Tammy in a rhythmic voice, and she fell into a relaxed state. I was mindful not to give her any pointed suggestions.

When she passed all the markers for being in a deep trance state, I gave her the suggestion she would go to the place that would give her the most healing at this time in her life.

Tammy soon found the place and time, and she raised her finger to signal she was there. I gave her the suggestion she would simply be an observer, without personally feeling pain or emotion, and if she came to a place of trauma she would report the event just like a reporter.

She entered into her place of healing, and began to recount her experience. She was eleven years old, and staying all night with a family we knew well. They had horses and Tammy was excited because the father promised to take her for a horse ride. Out the door she bounced ready to go; she couldn't wait to sit on the tall horse.

The father grabbed her by the arm and swung her up in front of him. He put his arms around her and said, "Giddy up," and the horse began to trot. The father squeezed his arms around her chest. He was hurting her, but she didn't want to fall off the horse, so she didn't say anything.

The two of them, came to a barn where the father stopped the horse. Another man came out from the door to greet them saying, "It's about time you got here."

She heard the father say, "Did you bring the video camera?"

He answered, "Does a bear shit in the woods?"

Tammy didn't like the way the other man smelled; he smelled like beer. Her daddy drank a beer every once in a while, but he never smelled like it. The father slid off the horse, and they all went into the barn. The barn smelled like dirt and hay. Tammy thought the barn was cool looking. She used to play in the barn at Grandma and Grandpa's house. It was a lot of fun.

There were four other men there; they called and jeered at the father. There were beer cans all over the floor of the barn. Tammy was beginning to feel a little nervous.

The father put Tammy in the circle of the men and said to her, "I want to show you a good time."

She wondered what he meant.

He began to touch her hair and then her face. His hands slid into her blouse. He began to unbutton it and Tammy said, "Don't." She slapped his hand away.

He whispered, "It's all right, I'm just going to show you a good time."

Tammy didn't think she wanted to have a good time. He

began touching her all over her body and Tammy tried to pull away. She began to yell, "Don't!"

The other men began hooting and hollering and then the father held her arms behind her back. He began to undress her and do things to her that hurt her. Tammy was confused and frightened at what was happening. Why was the father hurting her?

She heard the other men yelling, "Come on, get it done, it's our turn."

Tammy was yelling, crying, and fighting back but she couldn't stop them. A part of her left her body, so she couldn't feel the pain.

The master of darkness was lurking in the shadows while all of this went on. He saw the opportunity to snatch a part of Tammy's soul that had left her body. He grabbed it and ran, locking it in the cave of darkness where he keeps all children's souls who are raped. After the men were done with Tammy, the father put her on the horse and told her, "Don't tell anyone, they won't believe you anyway."

She believed him. When Tammy got back to the house, she ran into the bathroom and threw up. She washed herself repeatedly trying to wash off the sticky, icky feeling of shame. No matter how much she washed, the back tar of shame just wouldn't come off. She crawled into bed and cried and cried. She stayed silent for twenty-five years. The seeds of addiction had been planted, and all of our lives were changed forever.

I knew in my heart what I heard was true, although I know that there is the potential for confabulation under hypnosis. (Confabulation is a phenomenon where a subject under hypnosis makes something up, either knowingly or unknowingly, in response to a question.

As an example, this may occur when a subject who is

extremely relaxed is asked to remember information from a crime to which they were a witness. While the subject is attempting to recreate what he saw, the hypnotherapist begins to ask him questions that he cannot presently answer. Under pressure, the subject could make up an answer.)

A Mother's Poem

~Sharron Magyar

A hole in my heart-
As black as his anger.
Tears fall for my child.
Who was the monster who stole my child's soul?
A thief sucked out her life, laughing – taunting,
Throwing it into my face, raping my child
Of her innocence and dignity.
Shame now covering her body, hiding her pain.
Years searching, searching for the answer.
Who put this cloak of darkness upon her?
Answers elude me, who stole my child?

One time when I was riding in the car next to the same man, he brushed his hand against my breast and left it there. I pulled myself back out of his reach, and thought maybe I had imagined it, but I never forgot it. With sickening certainty, I began to think of all the girls in the neighborhood, as teenagers and then adults, who had grown up with alcohol and drug abuse problems. I suspected Tammy wasn't the only girl this man had raped. I needed proof for my peace of mind.

In one family I knew well, an older brother took care of his younger sister, and I suspected she had been also abused by the same man. Her substance abuse was so severe, the family was afraid she would kill herself. I called him and told him about Tammy, and asked if he thought there could be a possibility that his sister was raped by the same man.

He said he did think there could be a possibility, and I asked him to talk to his sister to see if she'd been raped at any time in her life. He didn't tell her what happened to Tammy. She told the same story as Tammy. She was ten. She was riding horses with a group of people. The same man cut her from the group of other riders, and pulled her off the trail. He raped her, and told her the same thing he told Tammy, "If you tell, no one will believe you."

I felt sick, but I had my answers, and so did her brother. I knew the day of their rape was the beginning of both of our girls' addictions. Dark entities had taken up residence in the place where the girl's soul parts had been snatched. So as not to be discovered at any cost, the dark ones hid. While hiding, they could wreck the girl's lives, and always pull them deeper and deeper into fear and addiction.

Consciously, Tammy didn't have a clue about what had happened, yet the trauma had been lying in her subconscious all those years.

I was sad for my daughter and for her friend, and I was angry, so very angry! Yet, Tammy and I both felt a strange sense of relief at finally knowing what had happened. Piece by piece, more information bubbled up to Tammy's awareness. Now what would we do with the information?

I visited Tammy at the prison every week, and we began talking about her feelings of shame and anger connected with the rape. What did she need to do now? Did she need to confront her abuser? It was twenty three years later.

These were all hard questions. There were families and children who could be negatively impacted by any decision she would make.

My Child

~Sharron Magyar

You're hiding in the shadow of my brain,

Every waking moment cloaked with your presence.

I can't allow my thoughts to land there,

Too much sadness to bear.

You were my child, yet I knew you not at all.

Secret thoughts as vile as cancer eating away your smile,

You'll always be there in my heart, a sadness tucked away.

Maybe one day I'll figure it all out, what happened?

Waiting for time to ease my pain.

Addiction: The Disease

There are a million books written about addiction. All have very sound advice, yet none of them seem to have any impact on people's ability to free themselves from addiction. I want to share what I have learned about addiction that pertains to the *energetic and spiritual* aspect of addiction. All that I have learned, I have learned though heartache and tears. Not one parent would choose for their child to be a drug addict, or an alcoholic, yet that's the journey some of us have to make.

At the very root of addiction is fear and shame. As long as a person with addiction is in denial, or disconnected from their emotions, they are powerless over the addiction. You may believe that anyone who is an addict should just stop doing it. If that were possible, there wouldn't be so many addicts walking around.

Addiction is a disease, the same as if a person has cancer. Just like cancer, it can simmer under the skin or the surface for a long time, until it erupts on the surface. Addiction, just like cancer, can kill you slowly or quickly, and there is no predicting the outcome. Often it is death. Just like some cancers are curable if you catch them in time, addiction is better treated early.

Biological and sociological factors are important with both cancer and addiction. For some people addiction is death, and for others they must learn to live with and care for it. Just like there are different stages of cancer, there are different stages of addiction. Each stage causes heartbreak and devastation for both the ill and addicted, as well as their families.

I kept asking God to show me clearly the nature of addiction. Some of the things I'll share with you are out of the box. My journey led me to learn more, much more. My daughter was dying of her addiction, and I was continually asking questions about the true nature of addiction. I invite you to step into a multi-sensory level of thinking so that you might consider addiction in a different framework.

Soul Fracturing

In almost every instance of severe addiction I have seen, the child has learned at an early age that a part of them can leave their body during extreme trauma, and move into a non-ordinary world. When a soul leaves their body, it is vulnerable to the attachment of dark energy. The master of dark energy can take a person's disconnected soul part into a cave of darkness to gather strength and power from its victim.

This power is then used to seduce the attached person into addiction. Flawed logic and damaged thinking then negatively influence the addict's beliefs, attitudes, and actions, both emotionally and physically. The impacted person is drawn further and further into lies and addiction. Their choices and opportunities become narrow, as they become a puppet of the dark energies.

Multiplying the problem, the dark energy that the addicted person is currently carrying, can also attract earthbound attachments, which enter through empty spaces or holes in a person's aura. These holes are created by addictive behavior, such as taking drugs or alcohol, or engaging in other negative addictive behavior. Thus the more a person drinks and takes drugs, the more distorted their energetic protection becomes. The weakened aura then allows negative energy to become trapped in the body, as well as attached to the body.

Negative energy attracts more negative energy; a vicious cycle is created. What is important to note is, if a person is attached to dark energy or spirit, it doesn't make the person evil. This dark energy has the potential to be removed and transformed into light.

Part of our journey through life is to experience the human condition of darkness, so that we can draw closer to the light and Higher Source through our intentions and choices. The lessons our souls want to learn can appear in the form of our experiences. Rising above addiction takes determination, faith, good intentions and choices.

To heal a person of addiction, the soul needs to be freed of all possessing earthbound and dark energy, for the healing to be lasting. Without releasing dark energy, the addict has a great possibility to be continually drawn back into addictive behavior regardless of their intentions. I do not believe this can be done without the help of the Higher Power of life, light and love. They are always stronger than dark energy.

Earthbound Entities

Human spirits who do not transition to the light or to dark after death, and remain on the earth plain, are earth bound entities. These spirits can attach or enter into a living person. When a person hosts an entity, they may feel the attached entity's thoughts, physical ailments, and addictions. The subconscious always knows the time when those feelings, ailments or addictions started. They will feel foreign to the host.

Why would a spirits attach to a living person? Earthbound spirits sometimes become lost and attach to a person out of their need for safety. They often have unresolved issues, are confused after death, aren't willing to let go of addiction, or they are full of anger. Sometimes spirits attach or enter a living person who is alive, in order to continue their addiction. A grandparent, parent or relative who has left a loved one on earth can attach out of their misguided desire to help a loved one, or to be around someone familiar. Finally, an earthbound entity can be tricked by dark energies into attaching and creating problems.

There are other reasons a person can be vulnerable to attachments besides addiction. The protective shield that surrounds the body may be down, possibly while in surgery, in jail, or in extreme states of fear. At other times the shield may be weakened due to illness. Being mindful to ask for protection from your Higher Source is beneficial.

Soul Exercise 18: Protection Prayer

Angel Protection

Among the ways to protect your energy field is to pray for protection to your Higher Power for assistance. As humans, our decisions and choices are made through our own free will. Because choices with free will are given, you must specifically ask for protection. Angels can remove all earthbound entities as well as dark energies from your body, aura and soul. They will also protect your home, workplace, and vehicle, if you ask.

The following is an angel protection prayer to use at least daily.

Give thanks to your higher power while inviting in your Spirit Guides, Angels, Archangels, and Ascended Masters to be present. Enter into prayer, and visualize a bright white light completely surrounding your body.

Invite your Angels to remove attachments to the body, aura and your entire being. Ask them to remove all earthbound, demon, or dark energies, and any other negative or inappropriate connections from your body, soul and energy field. Ask your Angels to cleanse, heal, and balance your energy centers. Ask Higher Beings for grace and to protect you.

Visualize the Angels filling and shielding you, your home, and your workplace with a brilliant white light surrounding you with love. Also visualize a glistening white light coming into the top of your head and filling your body. Ask the Angels to guide and direct you to be loving, caring, forgiving, and humble. Ask for every cell and organ to be cleansed.

State your intention to reject all the work of the dark ones. Vow to serve your Higher Power in all that you do and say. Ask that you may achieve your life's purpose as well as your gifts. End the prayer by thanking the Higher Power and Angels for their protection.

Lies

Think about all the people you know who may be suffering from addictions such as drugs, alcohol, pornography, excessive eating, smoking, etc. Addictions have a devastating effect on the individual's self-esteem. Even though these behaviors are self-destructive, people with addictions will engage in them repeatedly. At the root of addictions are lies. Addicts habitually lie to themselves and others. One lie leads to another in order to cover the first. Pretty soon they believe their own lies.

Tammy was addicted to drugs and she was also addicted to lying. She often couldn't tell her own truth from a lie. She felt so bad about herself all the time, that she always said what she thought others wanted to hear.

A liar can't fool people about lying. They only fool themselves in to thinking others don't know they are lying. Most people lie to avoid guilt and shame. On the surface it seems that lying displaces negative emotions. My observation is that lying forces guilt and shame into the subconscious mind.

Lying breaks people's trust. Once trust is broken, the

people who are lied to are disappointed that you didn't respect them, or yourself, enough to tell the truth. If you find yourself lying, stop and ask, "What uncomfortable feelings am I avoiding?" Dig deep into the root of the problem, and then figure out what is needed to make you feel better. Prayer, meditation, hypnosis, breathwork, and self-hypnosis can all help you make positive changes with your beliefs.

Have you ever looked into the eyes of someone who's gravely addicted to drugs? Their soullessness is reflected in their eyes. The seeds of their addiction were planted with just one lie. To recover the soul from addiction, lies must be taken back to break away from dysfunctional beliefs.

I'm not going to gamble anymore; I'm not going to overeat anymore; I'm not going to do drugs anymore; I'm not going to lie anymore, and I'll stop tomorrow, are all dysfunctional beliefs when you continue to do them. Breaking away from lying to yourself and others brings freedom.

10
Forgiveness

My daughter Tammy internalized being raped as, "I'm bad. I'm not good enough." For her and many people, this emotional reaction is the basis of many addictions. She lived her whole life feeling that something was wrong with her, and she was spinning on the merry-go-round of self-hatred. Fear entered her world; fear of men, fear of trusting, fear of feeling, and fear of being out of control.

Early in life Tammy learned the world was unsafe. She learned that drugs kept her from feeling, and kept her from being fearful. They promised relief, and lured her into feeling whole, thus the relentless cycle of addiction began. The central problem was, Tammy couldn't love nor forgive herself.

Many children deal with sexual abuse by splitting off parts of their personality. Each part has its own function. As an example, I have the artist part of me, the writer part of me, and the athletic part of me. These personalities are not always in operation, they come forward as the needs demand. For a child that has been sexually abused, one personality may be the victim and perhaps one personality carries anger.

The more traumatic the abuse, the more likely new personalities will be created. In energetic jargon these personalities would be considered soul fragmentation. In the psychological world these parts may be considered multiple personalities, when they gather enough power that they control a person's life.

Each person contains a protector personality whose strength is equal to the trauma they have experienced. In other words the more trauma experienced, the stronger and more predominate the protector is in a person's life. If you are going to do healing work with someone you must have co-operation with the protector, otherwise you will be hitting your head against a brick wall. Communication of your positive intentions can bring the protector on board.

Don't expect much direct communication with the protector. Their job is to protect and they do it silently and efficiently.

Energetic soul fragmentation can happen with physical, emotional, sexual or spiritual trauma. The fragmentation function is to survive trauma without destroying the person. Created personalities are generally not in an individual's conscious awareness. In extreme cases, trauma can cause total amnesia of the event. This was what had happened in my daughter's case, until the day of hypnosis. Tammy had frequent nightmares and migraines, but never consciously knew they were connected to the having been sexually abused.

Often, a formed personality that contains anger and hatred is the fuel for addiction. The energetic soul part must be reclaimed through soul retrieval before addiction can be addressed. In extreme cases, a shaman is needed to assist in retrieving the soul part prior to healing traumatic wounds.

The Thief

~Sharron Magyar

I'll lure you with a lie, ecstasy I promise, a respite for life.

Beautiful garments I wear of silk and sensuality,

You keep coming back for more.

Shame hidden deep inside, cloaked out of sight,

You need me to keep away the pain,

And then you're trapped in my sweet embrace.

Decay replaces the allure as your teeth and hair begin to rot,

And I am delight because I know,

I am closer to stealing your soul.

Empty eyes, empty heart, empty mind and empty soul,

I have drug you to my cave,

Making me the master, and you the slave.

I am a liar and a thief,

And you are no longer care.

Soul Exercise 19: Divine Forgiveness

Always do meditation in a relaxing, private place. You may tape record this meditation and play it back.

- ♥ *Pick a spot on the ceiling and stare at it until your eyes become tired. Take a deep breath. Breathe deeply into your belly for seven counts; hold your breath for seven counts, exhale for seven counts, and hold for seven counts. Repeat this process seven times. Focus on releasing all the negativity while exhaling. Breathe in tranquility and peace as you inhale. Breathe out stress and tension as you exhale. Eventually, you will step into a natural breathing rhythm and fall into a deep relaxation.*

- *Start at the top of your head, bring down the white light of energy into your body; bring it down around your eyes, relaxing the muscles around your eyes . . . . Bring the white light down to your throat; let it filter across your shoulders, and down to your hands. Let go of the tension in your shoulders, in your neck, relax those muscles.*

- *Breathe light into your heart, and imagine the light expanding bigger and bigger at the center of your heart. Push the light outside your heart, surrounding it like a nice glove . . . . As you breathe, feel love in your heart for yourself, your friends, your family, and the universe.*

- *Bring energy down to your solar plexus, and let the energy expand bigger and bigger . . . . contract the energy smaller and smaller, then expand it larger and larger until it starts flowing down through your pelvic area. . . . bring the white light down to your knees, to the calves of your legs, and to your feet. Imagine that you're doubling the relaxation you currently have.*

- *Give yourself permission to go inward . . . . . imagine that you see yourself standing in front of you . . . . You are healthy and whole and are radiating beautiful rainbow colors; that encompass your body . . . . Tell yourself you forgive yourself of any wrongdoing . . . . Allow yourself to let go of the past . . . . Release your emotional attachments . . . . Tell yourself you approve, and love yourself. . . .Ask your guardian angel to give you something symbolizing self-forgiveness.*

- *Visualize yourself surrounded in a bubble of love. Take another deep breath and feel your divine love. Feel centered, balanced and whole.*

- *Count from one to five, and then open your eyes becoming alert and aware.*

God's Grace

Sometimes lessons come from the most unexpected people. When I found out my daughter was raped by five men, several of whom I knew well, I felt anger welling up in my heart. I could think of all kinds of ways I might make them pay for what they did to my daughter. This daughter of mine, the one who was a drug addict all her life, knew what it was like to be judged. Through the entire struggle she bore a compassionate heart and knew how to forgive in spite of her wounds.

"Mom," she told me, "I don't want to be a victim for the rest of my life. I want to forgive. I don't want to be obsessed with the bad things that happened to me in the past. I intend to step out of the misery of my life, and not give the people who hurt me any power."

Forgiveness for me did not come so quickly or easily, it was a process. It was difficult for me to forgive because her rape was not a random act; it was a cold hearted act of deliberation. I had to ask myself the question, do I want to spend the rest of my life holding onto unforgiveness? Inability to forgive can lock you into negativity. How do I forgive? Every time I thought about how someone deliberately hurt my child I felt angry and sad.

The inability to forgive was harming me, my children, and my friendships. It was making me judgmental. It often flared up in the form of bitterness, and it held me in a state of resentment.

I finally set the intention to forgive. It's one thing to say you're going to forgive, but forgiveness does not always come easily or quickly. In my case, it was a process. I had the will to forgive, but there was a break between will and action.

I ultimately realized I'd have to ask for God's help to forgive. To do that, I would have to humble myself before God, and humbling myself was pretty distasteful. I realized refusing to forgive did not stop the pain, it spread it.

God finally moved me into a place of grace showing that if I held on to my resentments, my soul would become sicker and sicker. If at any time I felt unloving, I would give myself time to process. I had choices; I held onto my intention to forgive, and had faith in God to bring it about.

My intention to forgive did not mean that I was allowing the wrong doers to be unaccountable. The people that raped my daughter were wrong. They will have to get right with their Higher Power and with society. By asking God's help in forgiving, I discovered He gives us his grace to live with our most painful hurts and losses.

Focusing on forgiveness also forced me to take a good look at myself. In what areas in *my* life do I need to ask for forgiveness? You may want to ask yourself that question, too. There is humbleness in knowing we all have to bend our knees, to ask forgiveness for our shortcomings. And in the asking, huge growth is available to the soul.

The lesson in forgiveness taught me to give up control, and turn my anger, as well as my need to have control, over to Him. Lessons in having faith and in treating our relationships with grace were invaluable.

Forgiveness for the Family

On the home front, my family struggled with their feelings about Tammy. Each of us experienced mixed feelings. All of us were angry that Tammy (wouldn't or couldn't?) quit doing drugs. The family was angry because she hurt Steve and I, and her children. You can't even imagine the anger over her involvement with the fourteen year old boy. Due to the circumstances, it was understandable my family related to her from a place of judgment.

I was feeling the pressure of forty family members' unexpressed feelings projected onto me. The burden felt unbearable. Not only did the pressure of my family's feelings impact me, I felt the strain of public opinion as well. I was constantly being told "tell Tammy this or that" or "you need to just do this" or" do that." Everything was far too complicated for the simple solutions they offered. I prayed to get through all of it one piece; I was struggling.

Since a lot of my sisters and my one brother live out of state, we used a family website to communicate. It is a great way to stay apprised with what was happening with the family. I frequently thought about how the family related to Tammy.

Ultimately, I posted a letter on the website expressing my opinion that the only way the family communicated with Tammy was in judgment; that their love for her was conditional, the condition being that if she does all the things they think she should, then they will love her. Tammy already knew she could never live up to their expectations - no one had to tell her.

It took two weeks before I received any reply. When I did, you would have thought I had dropped a bomb in the middle of the family. All four of my sisters wrote, one by one, to tell me about everything they thought I had done wrong to cause the situation we were in. Every time another letter came, I would cry and cry. I dubbed the website the hate site. A part of me recognized a door opened to allow family members to express their feelings about Tammy, good or bad. Right now bad. I prayed each day, "God give me the strength and courage to see this through."

One part of me knew the opportunity for the family members to air their long silent feelings in an open forum was good. I allowed them to say what they needed without responding in any way. The gist of the posts was that it was entirely my fault Tammy turned out the way she did. I didn't defend myself. Neither did I agree, or disagree with them.

One comment was, "If you had raised Tammy like God wanted you to, she wouldn't have been a drug addict." Another comment was, "You shouldn't have done so much for her." I was fighting mad. They believed I should have or shouldn't have done something to prevent Tammy's addiction. I felt their comments were unjust. They simply didn't know I had no control over Tammy's addiction no matter what I did.

Most puzzling to me, they considered Steve blameless. Ah-ha, now I know what projection is. Together, Steve and I prayerfully made decisions connected with Tammy. We hoped that we were responding the way God would have us respond. Prayer gave me strength to give my family a safe place to vent their feelings, and not let it crush my spirit.

One part of me experienced all their projections, while

another part of me, my higher self, observed. When I was the experiencer, the ego stepped up, feeling hurt and mad. "I'll never forgive them for their harsh words," was my internal talk, along with all kinds of other crap. When, I made the transition to being the observer, I could understand their fears, anger, and ego - based reactions.

I had a choice, I could be the experiencer, and hold onto an angry heart, or I could be the observer, and have a compassionate heart. I chose a latter.

After all my sisters' feelings were thrown out into the open, the family moved toward forgiving Tammy. I am so grateful my family was brave enough to directly look at, and express their anger and hurt, because it was an important part of healing for both them and me. I once heard that a family's illness is equivalent to the secrets they keep. If that was the case, then our family had taken one huge step forward.

Did I enable Tammy? Yes. It took me twenty-five years to figure out enabling is doing something that prevents a person from getting his/her life lesson. As a parent, who loves their child, you don't want to turn your back on them, yet you should draw the line at destructive behavior. The better question for me should have been, if I take a particular action, would it prevent my child from learning her lesson on her own terms?

You can't rationalize or fix addiction. Many of the decisions Steve and I made weren't the best for Tammy, but we made them to protect the grandchildren.

There are things I would do differently, if I had my life to live over again. Life is a hard teacher. I can't wallow in guilt about the decisions we made. They were the best we knew, given the complexity of our situation. Steve and I also made some very good decisions. Our prayers helped us in making good choices for Tammy and her children.

Tammy's children experienced a great loss. We still loved Tammy, regardless of all her bad decisions and the pain she caused. She was our daughter. Personally and collectively we now put our focus on how to help Tammy, the family, and the children heal.

Soul Exercise 20: Letting Go of the Past

Tune into the idea of forgiveness. Become aware of what your body is telling you. Do you have a feeling of distress anyplace? Are there toxic memories or beliefs that cross your mind? Ask these questions of yourself.

Who has wounded you?

Who has gossiped about you?

What has happened in the past that still hurts?

What are you angry and resentful about?

What do you need to let go of?

Sometimes, just recognizing what you need from the person you want to forgive is the entry to forgiveness.

Journal: *Set the intention to forgive. What parts of your past do you need to let go of? Write and concentrate on the words and imagery they conjure. Make a list of the people you need to forgive; it can be a reminder to be working on forgiveness. Visualize the steps you need to take to restore your peace of mind through forgiveness. Journaling is personal and can create dramatic changes within.*

Forgiveness does not change the past, but it does enlarge the future.

~*Paul Boese*

11
Ancestors

For the Children

As Raymond and I continued working together on the book, I was beginning to see a snapshot of him as a wounded little boy who didn't have a chance in life. How he managed to survive his childhood trauma was beyond my comprehension. My respect for the street boy, who did what he needed to survive, was growing; he had guts and courage.

As Raymond recounted the story of his mother's death, I knew he had to be referred to a psychotherapist. Fortunately, he had previously worked with one and was able to get an appointment with her. Raymond's experience with counseling was better than Tammy's. He found a counselor who was wise and knew how to help him.

We continued with the book. When Raymond recounted his story of sexual abuse, I was ready to stop. Raymond was determined to continue. For the first time in his life he was able to share his story. We moved forward. He was seven years old when someone in his family sexually, emotionally, and mentally began abusing him. The abuser killed his gerbil, and threatened him saying if he didn't do what she told him to do; she would kill his brother like she killed his gerbil. All he knew, was she had killed his gerbil, so he knew she could kill his brother. Children are generally lied to and told, "If you tell, no one will believe you." They do not have the higher functioning mind to rationalize the truth from a lie.

I continued recording his story in picture language, while tape-recording the sessions. I was appalled at the cruelty he recounted, and was ready to quit. Raymond told me, "We have to think about the children the book will help; we can do it for the children." A very persuasive argument indeed. My art and the drawings were childlike with a compelling beauty and simplicity.

As we proceeded, I thought of every creative hypnosis suggestion I could use to help Raymond. This work was not for the faint of heart. Daily we worked. I drew as Raymond went into trance to tell his story. The two things we had going for us was trust and intention; trust that God was guiding and leading us, and our intention to create a book to help heal children who had been sexually abused.

This was going to be the ultimate "hero's" journey, a call to action and the beginning of transformation for both of us. I wanted to refuse that call, but I knew in my heart I was supposed to answer it. We had no idea of the challenges before us. Raymond certainly had more courage than I did. He would have to enter into the abyss, experience death and to battle the "dark one," before he could make atonement and transformations. What we didn't know at the time was that we would be rewarded with many gifts for accepting the challenge.

Many people from different walks of life were drawn into the creation of the story to help us. As Raymond stood on the threshold of the abyss; shame, anger, and pain floated up. Helpers began appearing both in the physical and the spirit world to prepare and guide us on our journey.

We were given a series of tests before we could begin transformation. Raymond was dying to his old world and transitioning into a new one. He had the courage and grit to look at his "cries in the night," and see the connections to his past lives. As he unpeeled each layer in his story the hold that drug's had on him began to loosen.

Grandfather

I didn't set out to learn past life regression, but it was about to become part of the journey Raymond and I were taking together. We were on a healing quest, and our paths were linked.

What I've learned about humans, is that we are so entrenched in living out our emotions that we block the flow of information from the bigger scheme of reality - our past lives, ancestors and archetypical patterns, as well as higher and lower energy levels. Are past lives provable? Not always. However, there have been documented cases of information connecting present lives with past lives.

A street boy with few manners, (although he did know how to honor the rules of living on the streets) Raymond could be stubborn and obstinate. He could also be funny, clever, charming, and so very smart. Lessons came for both of us and often centered on money, doing due diligence, being on time, and being impeccable with words and actions. We were being taught to have honor.

There were times while writing the book *Cries in the Night: Raymond's Story*; I would get exasperated with Raymond because he was stubborn about his lessons, meaning he had to get them again. Of course, that meant I had to get the lessons again, but stick it out I did. If we had to get a lesson the third time, it hurt like hell.

There were other times Raymond was at wits end with me because I could be demanding and tenacious. In the end, he had the courage to go inward through the pain so that he might claim the gifts God had given him. Above all, I had respect for his willingness to look at the dark areas of his life.

Recovery from years of molestation was a task few people ever manage, but he was working hard at it. Raymond and I were being used by a higher Power to write the book; I couldn't walk away from a book to help abused children. It had a hold on my life.

Raymond and I had been working together for about three months when we connected with a past life in which he was a shaman and a Native American Indian Chief. From what I could gather, he was a brave warrior with an air of arrogance, and he was quite a womanizer, breaking hearts along the way.

During our work on the book, we learned many things from the other side about the Native American way of life, including wisdom, valor, and courage. Their heart was in holistic healing, community, and the earth. Power for the Native Americans came from the inner-connectedness of man and creatures, as well as having honor and good character.

I have to laugh because there are a lot of new age books on how to "live in the moment." American Indians were well ahead of us in being today oriented, rather than goal-oriented. Learning about the Native American culture was positively impacting our personal beliefs and actions while providing personal growth to us.

Our world was about to change. The next past life regression took us to a life in which Raymond was a shaman in an ancient Peruvian culture. He had knowledge of drugs and herbs, and was both respected and feared. I was beginning to get the picture; Raymond was a shaman with a wealth of information about ancient shamanic lore.

You can imagine my surprise when he began speaking an Indian language under hypnosis. Although he had no understanding, or ability to speak a foreign language in his daily life, he spoke Spanish fluently from a Peruvian lifetime and Chippewa from another life time. The ability to speak a language a person had not been exposed to in this life is called Zenogloxy. I tape recorded all our sessions, many of Raymond speaking in Chippewa dialect.

We began zeroing in on a lifetime in which Raymond was a shaman in the American West, and an ancient Native American chief, "Grandfather," began showing up in our trance work. He was training Raymond to be a brave warrior with honor. Grandfather often talked to me in the Chippewa language.

Sometimes I understood what he was saying and sometimes I didn't, but I always got the essence of his teachings. He referred to me as the "one with a golden heart". As an aside, I thought it amusing that Grandfather's interactions with me reflected many of his cultural beliefs about women. I was expected to be reserved and have a closed mouth. I was very conscious of showing Grandfather respect.

Not only did Grandfather the chief show up, but his tribal warriors also came into our sessions. Many times the tribal council met, especially when Raymond was acting stupid or stubborn. The work we were doing in Raymond's current reality was somehow having an impact on the chief and his tribe in their reality. I suspected that Grandfather was Raymond in a past life.

Grandfather began teaching Raymond about the Higher Power, spirit animals and totems, the winds of the East, West, North and South. He also taught Raymond how to be a brave warrior who could recognize and fight evil. Grandfather was tough on Raymond when he needed to be. I began to figure out Raymond was being trained for battle.

Had I known what kind of battle, I would have quit right then and there. Raymond would take his soul back from the "dark one," which he had relinquished through his drug abuse. *Oh, for heaven's sake, I want out of this!*

Just as Raymond was given Grandfather, Raymond channeled Greta Alexander who was my spirit guide. She was a local psychic who had passed to the light about twenty years ago. She often spoke through Raymond and would advise me on how to help get him off drugs.

She instructed me to take care of myself through all the turmoil and she got on me if I started the pity-party thing, while always referring to "my golden heart" as Grandfather did. Of course by now, I figured out that Raymond is psychic, can communicate with people on the other side, and is a natural channel. I was having more conversations with people on the other side (including most of the thirteen deceased relatives I lost in one year) than I was having with my own live family.

I learned that Raymond's mom remained earthbound to stay close to him until we started working together. She then chose to go to the light after resolving some of her own issues. I spoke to all my aunts, uncles, and cousins related to my dad who had passed on. Almost all of them have transitioned to the light, except several uncles who clearly made a pact to give their soul to the "dark one." I learned that people who had sexually molested children were upon death immediately taken to the place for people who turn over their souls to the dark one. They are now under his rule; it's not a pretty place.

My ancestors were continually stepping in and out, giving me support or taking the opportunity to say hi, and not always the ones who had recently died. My grandfather, on my mother's side, who had been gone forty years connected with me. He was so surprised I was a grown woman: he still thought of me as a little girl.

Raymond showed my grandfather who was earth bound to the light. Many people who passed on and were looking to cross over into the light were drawn to us. I wished a million times I had kept a diary of all the people I talked to, and the reasons they were unable to cross over on their own. Everything I believed had been turned upside down. I knew in my heart there was a plan and a purpose for what we were doing, so we continued. The book was far bigger than Raymond and I.

Remember, for us the goal was to complete the book. I kept telling myself, "set your intention and follow through." Going forward Raymond was engaged in a battle to get off methamphetamines. He had to take his soul back; the going was rough, but he hung tight.

In the meantime, we were learning more and more about his role as a shaman. For shamans all over the world, illness is seen as a spiritual issue, a loss of the soul or diminishment of spiritual energy. Shamans are trained to retrieve lost soul parts by trekking into other worlds where parts are hidden. They perform soul retrieval in an altered state of consciousness.

Raymond was being taught to use his inner eye, to see in the dark, and to travel into different places in the spirit world to find information to help heal people. In addition, he was being trained to steal souls from the "dark one," a pursuit that is not for the faint of heart.

The work made us vulnerable to attacks from dark energies. Other trainings we received included our interconnectedness with all human beings, animals and plants. All living life has its own spiritual essence we can communicate and interact with. The following meditation was given to us by the ancestors.

Soul Exercise 21: Earth & Sun Meditation

Always do meditation in a relaxing, private place. You may tape record this meditation and play it back.

Take a deep breath. Breathe deeply into your belly for seven counts; hold your breath for seven counts; exhale for seven counts, and hold for seven counts. Repeat this process seven times. Focus on releasing all the negativity while exhaling. Breathe in tranquility and peace as you inhale. Breathe out stress and tension as you exhale. Eventually, you will step into a natural breathing rhythm and fall into a deep relaxation.

Relax deeply. . . . Let go of all your tension. . . . Notice all the sensations throughout your body. . . . Imagine yourself being cradled by the earth, while she cares for all your needs. . . . Place your attention on the firmness, support, and strength of the earth. . . . Imagine you and the earth are one.

Pull it into your feet. . . . Feel the energy rising from the earth and into your body. . . . As the earth energy enters through your feet, bring it up to the center and core of your body. . . . Unite the earth energy with the energy in your body. . . . Imagine the earth energy and your energy swirling, mixing with each other. . . . Receive her energy. . . . When your body is filled with earth energy stop, and rest. Send gratitude to the earth.

Now put your awareness toward the golden light from above. . . . Form a path from yourself to the golden warmth of the sun. . . . Allow the sun's energy to pour into the top of your head, bringing it downward to your very middle and core. . . . Allow this energy to merge and flow with energy present in your body. . . . Imagine the three energies flowing and melding together . . . . Earth, yours, and the sun . . . . Expand the energies, letting them grow bigger and bigger . . . . Feel the energy pulsating, replenishing, and saturating your whole body . . . . Then contract the energy, and bring it down to your center core.

When your body is fully saturated, stop and give gratitude to the sun and earth. Relish in the awareness of the energy. Count to five while bringing your awareness back to the room.

Through ancient rock paintings, history documents shamanism dating as far back as 10,000 to 30,000 years ago, to early humans. Explorers and anthropologists have evidence of shamanism in all corners of the world. Raymond and I began to have respect for the wisdom that has been passed down by shamanism throughout the ages.

The images I was drawing were piling up; some were disturbing, others a reflection of the divine. I began to see a correlation between my study of archetypical imagery and my drawings. The images were packed with powerful emotion. Have you heard the saying, a picture is worth a thousand words? I knew the artwork would illuminate the reader's subconscious mind, as well as the conscious mind. I was in attunement with the infinite; all time dissolved while I was drawing. I knew God was working through my art.

People from all walks of life suddenly started knocking on my door, calling, and asking, "Will you work with me? I've heard about your work with Raymond. Sometimes I worked with them by myself, and sometimes Raymond worked with us, applying his shamanic abilities. Being psychic gave him an uncanny knack for pinpointing how each person could be helped. For a shaman, lost soul parts live in a parallel existence or a non-ordinary world, or may be trapped in a fearful place. Raymond could locate and release any possessing entity. For every person healed in some manner, we personally took steps forward with the book.

As Raymond's story of abandonment, sexual abuse and drug addicted life became clear; my daughter's story of abuse was also unfolding. In prison, Grandfather of the spirit world began appearing to my daughter during her meditations. Both Raymond and I could feel dark energy breathing down our necks. I didn't know what the ending of the book would reveal.

Does Raymond take his soul back? Does my daughter rise above her addiction? Or do their negative life choices stay with them for life? Whatever the answer, the book was unfolding. I must be patient and patience is certainly one virtue I am working on in this lifetime.

At some point, I had to come to terms with the fact that the book was being directed by a Higher Power, not me. I had to let go of my own ego to write it. I am always goal oriented. Being so goal oriented was more of a hindrance in the book's case.

The more I would try to drive the writing of the book, the more resistance I encountered. I don't know how many times I had to get the lesson, "go with the flow." In time, I got it; let the book unfold as events were presented in real life. I was anxious for the end and a little afraid, yet, I knew a Higher Power was in control.

Out of nowhere, Raymond and I began spontaneously writing poems. People we were working with also began writing and bringing their poems to me. Many of them were about being abused. I just couldn't figure out how this was happening.

I can tell you that someone else had taken charge of my life, and I was just a pawn, and so was Raymond. I asked for permission to use many of the poems in the book. Everyone was delighted that perhaps they could help someone from going down the same road of shame and addiction that they had travelled.

Poems continued to come. I innately knew which poem went with each image I was drawing. I was continuously amazed at the visual and emotional impact each poem and image had; they went together like yin and yang. Our book was living a metaphorical life of its own. I was feeling stark raving crazy, because I could not rationalize all the synchronistic happenings.

While Tammy was still in prison, she drew images that came to her, and wrote poems about having been raped. Her images had a simplicity that was compelling. I then transferred her drawings into artwork. Tammy, who was intelligent, sensitive and gifted, wrote some of the poems in *Cries the Night: Raymond's Story*, while she was in prison.

At times writing the book was so rough that I thought I couldn't do it anymore. My sister, Nancy, gave me guidance when I got lost. Tammy kept encouraging us saying, "Mom, you're the only one I know that could tell the story the way it needs to be told." - So I became a storyteller. Steve was the rock that kept me grounded.

12 Past Life Regression

There are different layers of healing in the subconscious mind. Sometimes, it can be beneficial to start the healing process by connecting with past life regression. Healing and other gifts from your past life can be brought into your current life in an exponential way. I always tell my clients to judge the results, not the experience with past life regression.

Past life regression is for people who want to expand their life's experiences, connect with loved ones across the ages, draw upon their own wisdom, or bring to resolution past occurrences that are presently blocking their growth and happiness.

As you complete work in a past life, it can positively influence your current lifetime. Past life regression provides an opportunity to trace an issue to its origin, reprocess it, acknowledge emotions, and resolve relationship issues. By uncovering decisions made under duress in a past life, answers can be provided about beliefs that dictate your current life. Karmic debt from past lives can be balanced, particularly if you participated in acts against mankind, or were involved in dark energy or sorcery.

Past life regression not only can help resolve issues, but it can connect you with past life giftedness. Have you ever known someone who had a special giftedness from birth? An example would be a child who could play the piano beautifully from the moment they were big enough to reach the keyboard.

Musical giftedness could be a past life ability carried over into current life. You can connect with past lives to discover your special gifts, and bring the energy of the giftedness into your current life. (Raymond brought his giftedness of shamanic knowledge into this lifetime through past life regression.)

Some people think that regression is simply confabulation, but remember, the subconscious mind functions on a symbolic metaphoric level, not unlike the dream state. Even if the memories brought up are not true past life experiences, they can be useful to convey information to the conscious mind. (Any information obtained through a trance state regardless of content, can be a subconscious communication.)

It is a matter of deciphering the information. This subconscious information is similar to dreams in that sometimes it takes time to make sense of the information. Through hypnosis, imagery, dreams, or other states of deep relaxation, memories normally kept in the subconscious mind can be accessed.

Phobias and chronic physical ailments such as physical sensations and pains can have a past life connection. Fear of heights, claustrophobia, fear of spiders and snakes can be examples of past life phobias. Sometimes, these negative issues seem to persist into your current life, no matter how hard you try to change them. When you cannot logically explain why you have the pain or phobia, past life regression may be useful.

An intense attraction/aversion to another person can imply that the relationship has a past life connection. What is important is that the individual recognizes an unresolved problem, which has been carried over from a past life. Often, forgiveness releases past life relationship problems, and can positively influence a current life relationship.

The sequence that most people use when accessing past lives is first to identify their past life name, gender, age, along with the date and country where they lived. Some people can retrieve all the information, others little or sketchy parts of it. My observation has been that whatever information you need will be given to you.

While unfolding any traumatic events, staying in the body is an important part of the process. Sometimes the last thoughts or decisions a person make in a past life has a great impact on their current life. Most of the time after death, people see themselves being drawn to the white light and enter into it.

People experience past life regression differently. Some just have a knowing without visually seeing; others experience the lifetime as if they were watching a movie, while others feel it as if they and other people are literally having the experience. A few people experience both a current and a past life simultaneously in regression.

It is worth remembering that many autoimmune disorders, musculoskeletal symptoms, as well as psychosomatic symptoms often have their origins in past lives. Various current life issues can have their roots in unresolved soul wounds from past lives. Past life regression should always be done under the guidance and supervision of a certified past life regressionist. It is not a process to do on your own.

Rob

I began to realize somebody was going to have to write a poem from the view of the abuser for the book Raymond and I were working on. I couldn't imagine how that was going to happen, but the right person always seemed to be sent at the right time. This was one big lesson in trust for me. One day a young man gave me a call. He said, "I would like to make an appointment to be hypnotized."

I scheduled an appointment for him, but when I hung up I realized I didn't even know why he was seeking hypnosis. I knew for sure it would in some way pertain to the book, as that was the way life was unfolding at that time.

Rob and I became better acquainted as he sat in my office. We talked about his goals. He said he was interested in past life regression because he thought maybe it could help him find out what his headaches were about. Rob shared with me that all his life, he had suffered from cluster headaches that ran up the back of his neck, over the back of his head, and down to his eyes. He had even gone to Mayo Clinic to have a nerve removed to eliminate his pain, but he still felt the headaches weren't resolved.

We talked more about hypnosis in general and then began his hypnosis session. Rob easily relaxed and entered into a calm and comfortable altered state. Once he was grounded into the past life, I asked Rob to identify what he saw about himself. He began to describe his clothing as brown tie-up leather shoes, and a pair of pleated pants with a button up suit coat. From this information I assumed he was male. I then asked if he could tell me what town and country he lived in.

He replied, "Chicago, Illinois."

"What do you do for a living?" I asked.

"See my gun, I make collections," he replied. He acted out smoking a cigarette and squashed it under his shoe.

I asked him if he could recall his death, as if he were a newspaper reporter. He agreed and moved forward in time to his death. I explained to him that he didn't have to feel any pain or emotion; reporters just report. He began:

It is nighttime and I am with five of my buddies, waiting outside a bar for our boss. I am nervously looking around. Two cars drive up. Bullets are raining down on us. I feel a thump and burning fire at the back of my head. Pain begins to blur my vision and envelopes my body. Suddenly, I see myself lying on the ground as I float up above my body. With shock, I realize I am dead.

Before ending the regression I supported Rob as he asked forgiveness from people he had hurt, and then he asked forgiveness for himself in that lifetime. Rob brought that lifetime to completion.

When Rob walked out of the door, he had answers to a lifelong problem.

The next day Rob came back. I was not at my office, but my door was open. He came in and set a poem he had written on my desk. It was a poem from the abusers point of view. I never worked with him again

I began recognizing the multi-layering and multi-dimensionality of life in the spiritual world, along with the great potential regression has for healing the soul in the past and in the present.

Larry

One person Raymond and I worked with who stands out in my mind was Larry Creviston. Larry came for a free half-hour session to talk to me about past life regression.

Larry had a distinctive self-confident carriage. He was tall, well built, with intelligent eyes. His body looked tough as steel, in excellent physical shape. He had a handlebar mustache which seemed out of step with the times. As we built a rapport, I learned that Larry was a musician. He could play many instruments seemingly from birth, and often played bagpipes and taps during funerals at Camp Butler.

I asked Larry why he was interested in past life regression. He told me he thought he had fleeting memories of some of his past lives. Periodically he would get the overwhelming feeling that he had the sorrow of the world on his shoulders, particularly when he played at Camp Butler. He just couldn't figure out where the feelings came from. He was happily married and loved his job. He had researched the internet for information about past lives and decided to explore his.

Larry registered high on his suggestibility test. Since he had some spontaneous bleed through memories, I thought that past life regression would be easy for him. It was.

First Session: Through hypnosis and guided imagery, Larry entered into a deep level of relaxation where memories that were normally in the subconscious could be accessed. Visiting his first past life, he saw himself as a young boy in a poor household. At about age ten, a group of militia came to his house. Larry saw his father talking to the man in charge of the group. The next thing Larry knew, he was instructed to go with the men. His father told him he was going to live with them from now on. Larry didn't want to leave his father and mother.

Larry's father took him aside, and explained to him he did not have money to feed him. The military would see to it he was fed. Larry understood, but was saddened and overwhelmed with grief. Crying, he got on a horse behind one of the other men. He knew he was doing what his father wanted him to do; he would be a big boy like his father asked.

Larry was perpetually homesick for his home and family; he loved his parents. He spent that whole life in the militia, battle weary and fatigued. His only solace was playing his drum. Larry carried emotional scars of abandonment which settled in as an underlying sadness that transferred to his next life. I supported Larry in releasing and diffusing the energy and emotional blockages from that lifetime.

Second Session: Larry easily regressed back to another past life where he lived in a forest in Europe, perhaps

Germany, with his wife and children. He saw himself as a man walking through the trees. He relished in the quiet and smell of the forest. He was proud of where he lived, and proud of the home he had carved with his own hands for his family.

One day, returning home from the forest, he began to smell smoke. It looked like it was coming from the area of his house and he started running toward his home to see what was happening. When he came upon the clearing, all he saw was embers and smoke. Raiders had burned his house to the ground. His wife and children lay in the ashes. The memory imprinted on his mind and body. Grief rendered Larry hollow and lifeless for the rest of that lifetime. Several years after the fire, Larry joined the militia. Often, solders could hear his music echoing his melancholy and grief through night air.

I asked Larry to use his imagination and call his wife in the session. He was able to tell her that he was sorry for not being there to save her. Larry was able to bring a successful closure to that life, coming to terms with his guilt and grief that had weighed on him throughout his current life.

Third session: I saw a pattern in Larry's past lives, but felt there was more to the story than met the eye, so I asked Larry if it would be okay to call Raymond to join us in the next regression. I wanted the benefit of Raymond's shamanic ability to see what was going on energetically with Larry. Larry and Raymond easily dropped down into a relaxed trance.

Raymond began, *I see you as a soldier in many of your lifetimes. You always rose to a high level of achievement. Sometimes, you have been hard and mercenary. You've had a lot of loss and pain, but you gained strength and knowledge through the pain.*

You have soldiers here who have not crossed over into the light. They want to talk to you and thank you now. They want you to hear that your bagpipes and taps draw them to you, and open the door for them to cross over into the light to the other side. They are grateful for your music and willingness to be there for them.

The message for Larry was that his music had a purpose in the spirit world, as well as in the physical world. Raymond said the spokesperson and many of the soldiers bound to earth then chose to cross over into the light.

Larry's Comments:

"I would have feelings when I played my bagpipes that my personal space was being crowded. I discovered that there were spirits gathered around me to hear my playing. I also learned how to control that by picking someone who had passed away to mind the door to only let so many in. That helped quite a bit with my feelings of being overwhelmed when I play my music.

I also asked Sharron if it was possible to have physical ailments in this life carried over from past lives. Amazingly through hypnosis, back pain I had most of my life was cleared up once we found out how the wound had been inflicted in a past life. My back has not bothered me since.

As far as where I am going with this I don't know, my journey has not ended. I do know if I could use the word pressure, although that's not correct, a lot has been relieved and released through understanding and knowing what was causing it. I actually was able to get rid of the unnecessary burden I was carrying around.

I had felt strongly before about past lives because of connections with items and places. I didn't know exactly what it was. Sometimes I felt disconnected from the world, and other times I thought everyone else was disconnected. Through hypnosis I found out I wasn't off track. I have learned to manage better, and hope to manage better in the future."

Tammy and Raymond

At the same time Tammy was working hard on her own issues of sexual abuse, Raymond was working hard to comprehend his own abuse issues. Raymond's choice of drugs had been methamphetamine - an ugly drug; very few people free themselves of meth. If they do, the toll it takes on the body is devastating. Raymond was drug free, but it was a fragile line he was holding, and I knew it.

So many synchronicities were occurring in my life, I couldn't even begin to name them all. Books were dropped in my lap. People would call when I needed help with something. Money appeared when I needed it. Time would be cleared away if I needed it.

Both Raymond and I were making a huge transition. We were learning to trust God to provide for our every need; some were being met before I even thought of them. The more we trusted God, the more the "dark one" tried to trip us up.

My life was turned upside down. I would get up in the darkness of the night so I could work on the book from three to six in the morning without distractions, and then I would go back to bed. Sometimes I would go to sleep just to be awakened an hour later to write a poem. It was difficult to balance real life and my book life. Along with that, the shamanic work that Raymond and I were doing together had taken a life of its own.

Steve was cool and calm in the midst of all the people being drawn to our door. He listened; he gave me helpful advice, and he kept things running smoothly at the house. Sometimes he answered the phones so I could work. He took me out in the boat where I wouldn't be interrupted with my writing. He fished; I wrote.

He didn't understand all that was going on with the book, and for that matter, neither did I. Steve and I was both gaining respect for what was happening. Our house had turned into a revolving door. Through it all, we hung onto our sense of humor.

Tammy had done a lot of healing since entering prison. While there she was given the wrong prescription for her eye. It was two weeks before she discovered the mistake, and the medicine caused her to go blind in her bad eye.

The eye glazed over. She struggled continually with eye pain, and often became nauseated when the pressure got high in it. Eye problems had now become part of her life. Her eye was so disfiguring that people often stared at her. She was candid with everyone; she dealt with it better than I could have.

Time was quickly coming for her release from prison. It had taken hard work and guts to push forward. She'd gained a lot of respect from the family, and especially from Steve and me.

Ray and I continued to work on the book day after day. Both of us were wearing down. It had been one heck of a struggle for both of us.

One day, someone from the past named Mike appeared at Raymond's door, and proceeded to move in. I didn't have a good feeling about him; he couldn't look me in the face and that made me very uncomfortable. Once he arrived, Mike never left Ray's house, and a lot of strange people started to show up there. One day I confronted Raymond to find out if he was doing drugs again. He denied it. I knew he was lying. How did he think he could fool a mother of a daughter who was a drug addict?

Four months after Tammy was paroled, Raymond was arrested for manufacturing meth. Just like that, he stepped back into the drug world. Raymond was sentenced to six years at the Illinois State Department of Corrections.

I went to visit Raymond each week in prison, and we continued working on the book throughout his term. During his stay, Raymond entered the drug rehab program. He was learning about addiction, learning to be accountable, and to love himself. We both prayed that he could now stay free of meth.

Tammy was out of prison; Raymond was in prison. On the home front, Steve and I had taken on raising an angry grandson, who had built up a wall so high we couldn't pierce it in any way, and who could blame him? I swear Stephen Ray was a carbon copy of his father, even though he had not been around him while he was growing up. Stephen Ray had his own healing journey to make. I just hoped that he would quickly learn that he didn't have to be a victim all his life and that he could choose a beautiful life.

Try Again

~Sharron Magyar

Tears and fears cried, and years gone by,
While you're here regrets, do you still love me?
Smiles with you a while, time slipping by so fast

What's lost? Loneliness yearning for home,

Empty holidays alone again.

The sadness is I put myself in the pen,

Time slipping away each day into years,

You've grown; I've missed you so much.

Outside, inside, wishing I could do it all over again,

That's the pen.

Another chance, holding tight, walking right;

Get it right this time.

Stephanie had always lived in the shadow of Tammy's addiction. While Tammy was in prison, Stephanie and her husband Chad, took over raising Tammy's youngest child, Cheyenne. Stephanie was progressing forward in forgiveness and acceptance, determined to do it for Cheyenne's sake.

Everyday each of us lived with the shame Tammy put on us, and we discovered that shame can only destroy you if you let it. My family had grown in compassion and forgiveness.

When Tammy was released from prison, she couldn't find a job anywhere because she was now a convicted sex offender. There are different categories for sex offenders in the United States, and Tammy had been classified unlikely to offend again. Still, Tammy had a problem. First, most of the public believe all sex offenders are pedophiles. Second, the public believes once a sex offender, always a sex offender.

The truth is not all sex offenders are pedophiles. A person can become categorized as a sex offender if they urinate publicly, or if a nineteen year old has sex with a seventeen year old. Maybe time will educate the public that there is a wide range of illness between the different categories.

Statistically, it is likely that once you have been imprisoned, you will return again. Felons have a terrible time re-entering society, acquiring jobs and homes. Legitimate ways of earning a living are slim to none for a convicted sex offender.

Tammy finally got a job taking care of an uncle of mine who was a severe diabetic with an amputated leg. She and her youngest daughter, Cheyenne, lived with him and adjusted nicely. Cheyenne was thrilled to be with her mother again.

We kept Stephen Ray with us and they often saw each other. We felt it was best for both of them; we knew Tammy wasn't ready to take on an angry son. Tammy went to her AA meetings, and was careful to fulfill all her parole commitments. She eventually landed a part-time job at a grocery store. Her boss knew of her past; she told her to keep it between the two of them. Tammy had been working at the store for about a year. She liked it there and they liked her a lot. I began thinking that she could provide a normal life for herself and Cheyenne.

One day the grocery store got a new manager and Tammy was immediately called into the office. Her new boss fired her on the spot, because she was a registered sex offender. Tammy was heartbroken. After remembering she belonged to the Union, I suggested she contact them.

Originally, the Union representative told her they would fight for her, but later changed their minds. I just don't think they wanted to get involved in the sex offender thing. Tammy was left with no recourse. Shortly after the store event, my uncle died. Tammy was now without a job and homeless.

Steve and I purchased a trailer nearby for Tammy and Cheyenne so we could be close. Once again, we took on the bulk of support for Tammy; we felt we had no choice. How could we turn our back on our child, and our grandchildren? What was the fine line between enabling and loving? What would God have us do? We loved and supported her in all ways so she could put her life back together again.

Tammy and Cheyenne were excited about having their own place. Wherever Tammy lived, she had to register at the town's police station as a sex offender. Within three months of living in Chatham, Tammy was pulled over by the same cop five times. Every time he pulled her over, they towed her car. Tammy didn't have any money, so each time it cost Steve and I one-hundred seventy-five dollars to get her car out of impound.

One day when Tammy was driving home from the grocery store, she looked up and again saw the police lights behind her. The policeman told Tammy and Cheyenne, who was nine at the time, to step out of the car. Tammy explained once again that she had paperwork in her purse to prove her registration and insurance coverage.

The cop said, "I don't care what you have in your purse," and he called the tow truck. Tammy asked, "Can't I just take the car home, its two blocks away and you can follow me so I can get the groceries out. He said, "No, you walk."

Tammy and Cheyenne walked, both lugging their groceries all the way home. Once again we had to bail out the car. This was the final straw for Steve. When he found out Cheyenne had to walk home lugging groceries, he paid a visit to the chief of police. Steve told the chief of police that if the harassment continued, he would pursue a lawsuit against the police department. Tammy was never pulled over by the policeman again. Our lives began to settle into a nice boring routine, and we all breathed a sigh of relief.

Three and a half years later, Raymond was released from prison. He had been in the drug rehab program throughout his prison stay. He learned a lot about addiction and leadership. I continued working with him, and he seemed determined to live his life drug free. In the spirit world, the "dark one" tried to snag him every chance he got. We were smack dab in the middle of the battle between darkness and light. "The dark one" tried to keep him on drugs, and then tried to lure him back to drugs, knowing it would silence his voice. Raymond was now well trained by Grandfather.

Raymond had moved into a realm where he connected with angels, ascended masters, and spirit guides, who gave him unbelievable tools and gifts to use in his shamanic work. God kept holding onto and testing him, "Will you be faithful to me? Will you obey me? You have free will; you can make choices, what are your choices?"

The "dark one," on the other hand, tried to take away Raymond's free will, operating through fear, lies, and addiction. If he could keep Raymond in fear and addiction, then he could keep his soul, and he desperately wanted to keep Raymond's soul.

Angels

Our growth was happening at a phenomenal rate. We were learning that man can only be conscious, non-judging, and loving when there are no attachments or expectations. This would bring us to healing. Through the creation of *Cries in the Night: Raymond's Story*, we were making connections with higher beings to accomplish our task. It was surprising and delightful.

In the spirit world Archangel Michael often assisted us in the battles with the "dark one." He was huge and a force to be reckoned with. We learned we could call on other angels in any healing work that involved spirit release and house clearing. Angels were sent to us to help cleanse ourselves and others. We also found we had our own individual guardian angels assigned to work with us throughout our life. Angels only help if you ask for their help. God's Angels are a force that is positive, good and true.

We were given assistance from many different avenues to continue our work. We had daily contact with our highly advanced spirit guides, the ones who stay with us throughout our lifetime. Ancestors can often be spirit guides to us, like Grandfather is to Raymond. Information about Raymond's role as a shaman unfolded as time went on. He learned to use the potential of his mind, calling on spiritual helpers to heal the afflicted. Raymond was mediating between the world of people and the world of spirits. His primary job was to heal souls through soul retrieval.

The richness that accompanies the integration of opposites leads to opening doors to the true beauty of life. It doesn't matter how you think of it, whether it's higher power/lower power, darkness/light, detachment/attachment; the yin/yang of life brings us into its fullness. Opposing components of light and dark must be integrated by looking at your shadow side (the unconscious part of you that your conscious ego does not see). The negative part of the shadow tends to deny or remain ignorant of the least desirable aspects of one's personality. Positive aspects may also stay hidden in one's shadow.

We were determined to walk through the door of freedom by stepping out of fear and trusting God.

Tammy

Today I started writing the things I'm grateful for, and pulled out a journal my brother once gave me for Christmas. I opened the book only to discover I had sent the journal to Tammy while she was in prison. I had no idea how the book survived, since guards often confiscate journals. The following is Tammy's first page entry:

I'm sitting here at Lincoln Land Correctional Center; three days shy of being incarcerated for one year. I have learned a great deal during my time here. I am an addict, and I would never have committed crimes if I weren't involved in drugs. Even though this is the most terrible thing I've ever experienced, I truly believe that God wants me here so I can begin my true path in life. I'm coming into myself, and I have discovered that God has given me many gifts.

I am a healer, I use my hands. I can see a person's aura and feel their pain and joy. Sometimes it's overwhelming like a lightning bolt and sometimes it's very subtle. I know all is a process of becoming who I am meant to be. I have discovered a true relationship with my parents for which I'm grateful. I will be the mother to my kids as I was meant to be, when I go home.

My kids, God, I miss them so much it hurts. I regret so much that I have hurt the people that I love. Lord, please forgive me; I never want to see another drug for as long as I live. That includes all my future lives, too. I see so much pain and destruction on a daily basis, and shudder to think that was me. Finally, I'm starting to like myself for the first time. I want so much more out of life for my family and me. I would take all their pain in a heartbeat. I get out September 15, and it can't come soon enough, but I know when God decides it's time for me to go I will.

Three years after Tammy got out of prison; she got up one morning and fell in the bathroom. Her ten year old daughter, Cheyenne, heard her fall and ran to the bathroom. She knew Tammy wasn't breathing and tried to give her CPR. When she realized that wasn't working, she called 911.

The emergency squad rushed Tammy to the hospital and put her on life support. After two days and many prayers, we decided Tammy had suffered enough. We made the decision to take her off life support and Tammy died an hour later.

Tammy never drank alcohol at any time in her life, except in the last several years. She approached alcohol addictively, just like drugs. In the last year of her life I knew Tammy was drinking. I also suspected she had started doing drugs again. The autopsy report stated Tammy died from methadone poisoning, which stopped her heart.

In the very same year I lost my daughter, my father also passed away; thirteen of my other relatives also died; I was hit by a car while walking; my mother was diagnosed and had major surgery for thyroid cancer. The emotional and physical pain was indescribable, but through it all, there was hope. I hung on knowing that God had a purpose for my life.

## 13

The Golden Eagle

Today is Mother's Day

~Sharron Magyar

I remember holding her in my arms
She smiled with such charm
From my heart to her heart
Laughing eyes, curiosity from the start.
Today is Mother's Day
Such a mixture of love and pain
Someone cloaked my child in shame
Drugs and addiction trying to hide the pain.
Today is Mother's Day
My heart beating, still love and pain
Because I know each year will come
And I'll never see my daughter again.
Her heart robbed by deceit
Today is Mother's Day, one heart, one beat.

Grief

There is no way to describe the shock that one day your child is living, and the next day she has died. Never mind the circumstances. First, there was mind-boggling numbness. I could not feel anything except denial. It couldn't be true that my daughter was dead. I was living a nightmare. I couldn't think or take care of my body, or act reasonably with anyone.

Inane comments people made out of their own pain and discomfort just made things worse. I had not lost my mind, so why would they say such stupid things to me like, "I understand how you feel," or, "She is better off now."

Like hell you understand how I feel. All of my energy was sucked out of my body. It took enormous effort to walk from one room to another. Six months passed before my mind, body and emotions began to awaken; pain was all there was. I cried and cried until there were no more tears.

I wanted to die. Most of my tears were shed in the house and alone. I was ashamed to let anyone see my vulnerability. But not always - one beautiful spring day I went to McDonald's to get some breakfast. While I sat eating my sandwich, a memory of Tammy snuck up on me.

Out of the blue I started crying. I felt my face fill with shame because I couldn't control the tears. To make matters worse, a good friend from out of town was there, and he came over to comfort me. Again, I felt embarrassed and ashamed that I'd put him in the position to feel badly. I could give myself permission to deal with my feelings, but it was hard to compound my feelings with those of other people.

Grieving was taking its toll on my mind and body. I could not focus on anything for any length of time. Lethargy began settle in. I had hardly enough energy to get dressed or cook a meal, let alone think clearly about anything.

I forgot about appointments and to pay the bills. Spiritually, I checked out of my body. I wanted to be mad at God, but a part of me knew He knew what was best for Tammy. Ah, those well-meaning friends were right when they said her suffering was over. I just wasn't ready to hear it. It still didn't make the pain go away. I began to realize I had to surrender to my grief.

Some days I thought I was going crazy. I would be fine one moment, and on my knees the next. The unpredictability of grief was driving me nuts. I expected the emotional component, but not the physical devastation; it left me uncentered and debilitated. My heart was broken, and I didn't know how to put it back together again. I prayed my life would not stay stuck, and that God would find a way to get me through it.

> There is sacredness in tears. They are not the mark of weakness but of power.
>
> They speak more eloquently than 10,000 tongues.
>
> They are the messengers of overwhelming grief and unspeakable love.
>
> ~ Washington Irving

Tears

~Sharron Magyar

I woke up this morning with tears in my eyes,

It hurt in my chest and I need to cry.

Emotions I can't trust expressing the pain,

My heart's weeping again.

I woke up with tears in my eyes,

Holding my heart to protect it from its own pain,

I've remembered you're gone again

I woke up this morning with tears in my eyes,

Sadness overwhelming, grief to stay.

I'll brush away the tears,

Loneliness my companion.

I finally got out from under the shock enough to realize I needed a way to express my pain. Again I was led back to writing. As I told Tammy's story and the story of my journey with her, I began to see the light in the world. I cried a million tears; my heart was torn into a million pieces. I was gentle and patient with myself. If I needed to sleep, I slept.

If I didn't feel like being social, I didn't apologize. I simply had to do what I had to do to survive.

I made an effort to eat right and exercise as much as I was able. I was unbelievably selfish. All I could manage was to focus on my needs; I simply didn't have the energy to reach out to my friends. Dealing with their grief as well as mine, was like asking someone who had cancer to get out of bed and take care of a friend that had the flu.

All I could do was give myself permission to experience the pain, and not allow myself to fall into the "what if" trap. I was in survival mode, trying to put the pieces back together again.

Grief for Steve took a different track. The house that Tammy and her kids had once lived in needed to be sold. Steve began gutting and remodeling the interior. I realize now how important it was for him to have something he could single mindedly focus on. He spent nine months working in the house. If he felt like crying, he could cry.

He benefited greatly by keeping his hands and body busy. The house also provided a place for him when he needed to be alone. He could come back into contact and connect with people on his own terms.

Steve and I came together somewhere between my isolation and his. We talked and worked through our sadness. Sometimes we just sat together saying nothing. The rawness has now somewhat diminished. We still have moments and words that touch the sadness, but they are only moments, and they pass. Mother's Day, Father's Day and holidays are hard.

We have had to question what traditions to change in order to put ourselves in a better place. For the first time, we chose not to spend Thanksgiving with my sisters, and brother, and their families the year Tammy died.

Steve and I, Stephanie's family, and Stephen, were together at Stephanie's house. It would have been too overwhelming to deal with forty different people's feelings over dinner. Did my family understand? Maybe, maybe not, but they did support us.

We allowed ourselves to be surrounded by loved ones when we could; it was okay that it was not always. All I could do was cling to the hope that it would get better, and that there would be a time when I would find some degree of joy in my life again. My life had been changed forever. I realized I couldn't ever fill the void left by my daughter's death, but I prayed I would learn to live with it in a meaningful way.

I had no choice but to trust in the grief process. I clung to the hope that I would survive, and prayed that God had plans for my life. It was hard to see those plans from the darkness. Just when I thought things were getting better, a deep depression descended upon me, and I couldn't remember anything. Doom and gloom filled my thoughts; I couldn't see anything positive about life.

One part of me observed, "So this is what deep depression is like," while another part of me lived in it. I went to the doctor and he put me on an antidepressant. My body again said, "No way!" I was in a dark hole and couldn't climb out by myself. I had to hold on to faith that I would work through the depression. I prayed each day for God to lift the depression. Slowly, He did.

Transformation happened. I still have moments when grief springs up unexpectedly, but they are fewer and fewer. I remember the good times with my daughter with happiness, and I let go of the sorrow she brought into my life. I am free from the pain of seeing her suffer from addiction, and from my being helpless to prevent it.

My daughter is liberated from the pain of her life on earth, no longer enslaved to her life struggle with addiction. Learning to forgive was extremely meaningful for her. I have empathy and understanding for people in a dark place that they cannot escape. Now I can recognize grief in others, whether it's grieving the loss of a person, or the loss of something in a person's life. I thank God for the blessings that rise out of the pain. I wear my newfound wisdom with humility.

The Healing Power of Sound

I had three episodes of waking up in the morning with a pain squeezing in the center of my chest and radiating into my right breast. I ruled out problems on the medical end with my doctor, so I was now ready to explore more healing through sound therapy.

I explained the painful constriction in my chest to Teri, and she asked me if I could key into an emotional component. The only word I could come up with was grief; however that didn't feel accurate. I was sure that whatever it was would unfold through the session.

Lying on the massage table, Teri played an instrument that made a curious sound that I couldn't recognize; the instrument sounded like scratching paper. I was confused because I couldn't identify the sound, or where it was coming from. Finally I just relaxed, gave up trying, and entered a deeply relaxed state.

Teri entered into the spirit world and told me that my daughter, Tammy, was there and wanted to connect to me.

I was surprised. I always know that Tammy watches over me from the other side, but this felt like a special meeting arranged for us in altered state. I allowed myself to make contact, and was grateful to be with her. I asked her, "Are you pleased with the book?" She told me that she was very happy, and that it would help many people. (Even though Tammy had passed away, I often worried that Tammy would think I portrayed her negatively. In this energetic space she reassured me the book was exactly as it is supposed to be.) I breathed a sigh of relief, because I do not ever want to hurt my daughter. I felt comforted.

Teri then told me to call someone in for balance. I called my father. He is a steady mind and hand. Teri continued drumming and playing the chimes, while my feelings began to float up. My reflex was to swallow down the emotions connected with the energy, but then I realized the opposite was needed. I sat the intention to let the emotion up and out.

The emotion was now identifiable; it was regret. I was experiencing a profound feeling of loss and disappointment. The regret was not particularly personal, like I regretted doing or not doing something, it was more global. It was regret that Tammy had to suffer so much in her life, regret that my grandchildren were so impacted, regret that Steve and I had to go through so much, regret for what the rest of my family had to experience.

To let go of the regret, I had to let go of all of my disappointments about the past as well as the present. As Teri played her instruments, I gave myself permission to feel and observe the regret, until it cycled through my body and all of the emotion was spent. I breathed deeply and fell into a profound calm.

Teri then told me she had a message from my Dad's farmer friend. His message was, "Life is sometimes like being a farmer. You have to get into the muck with the pigs

MY GOLDEN HEART PUTTING THE PIECES BACK TOGETHER AGAIN

which are smelly and stinky, but around the corner is the sunrise." Well the pig metaphor is pretty disgusting; I knew about pigs since I grew up as a farm girl.

I instantly latched onto the sunrise.

> Regret for the things we did can be tempered by time; it is regret for the things we did not do that is inconsolable.
>
> ~ Sidney Smith

Tammy

~Sharron Magyar

What could have been; what should have been,

A little girl with a great big smile,

Eyes dancing all the while,

Someone stole her soul, her smile going cold.

A kiss for a puppy or kitten, while she hides her pain,

Her secret brings her shame.

Dancing eyes, sparking smile, drugs to hide a while,

Trying to find a way to run,

Innocence gone, can't change.

Addiction in its place, holding, never let go,

Happiness long life and a smile.

What could have been; what should have been.

The Golden Eagle

I was at my next sound therapy. I was very tired and didn't know if sound therapy would be helpful that night. Teri asked me to lie on the table; take a deep breath, and get relaxed and comfortable. My intention was to work on the energy connected with organization and prioritizing which had escaped me after the accident.

Teri put little beads at specific pressure points in my ears. One area was tender. She said it connected with the spleen which is also associated with the autoimmune system. Go figure, since I have an autoimmune disease. She began our session by playing different tuning forks right next to my ears. Some of the sounds were pleasant, some not so pleasant. Teri then alternately placed the tuning forks near my ears and on my big toes.

My body was totally immersed in sound. When she touched a place on my chest with the tuning fork, it was sensitive and tender. She told me it was another sensitive autoimmune point. I took in the music and listened with curiosity as I felt different responses in my body. After about fifteen minutes of sound therapy using tuning forks, Teri asked if I was feeling grief about anything.

My answer to her was, "I don't know if I do."

She said, "Check your body. What are you feeling in your body?"

I felt a tightening in my throat, a restriction, and curiously I didn't understand what it was. Teri asked me to focus on the tightness. Feelings began to expand around my throat. They grew bigger and bigger, expanding with vibration.

My whole body began to shake. I started to feel grief; tears began to stream down my face. I realized this was grief so deep I couldn't talk about it. While I was crying, I began to understand this grief came from taking my daughter off life support. I felt so alone in that decision; it broke my heart. I cried out all the emotion. While Teri continued with sounds of the tuning forks, I could feel the energy of my body re-aligning

Teri said, "There is a big bird coming in that's bringing in new energy." She visualized the bird's beak and claws in my hands and feet. "The energy will be used for the book." I was curious about this bird. Where did it come from, and what did it mean to me? When I later asked Raymond, he said, "It's a golden eagle."

Welcome golden eagle; let's see what energy it brings me.

> The pain passes but the beauty remains.
>
> ~Pierre Augusta Renoir

30 Days to Live

Steve and I went to Alabama to say our goodbye's to Tammy as we put her ashes in the Gulf of Mexico. She loved the ocean. We try to go there each year for a month; to enjoy the water and the low key environment. While we were there, red sores appeared around my nails on my hands. They felt like boils on my fingertips. This was the third time they had surfaced. My general doctor had already sent me to several specialists for blood tests and such, but they showed nothing.

When we got home, I again saw the specialist. This time I got a phone call, "We want you to come in for a consultation for the results on the blood tests." I was a little nervous; I didn't have a good feeling about what he would say.

The Doctor explained that this time the blood test showed that I have Dermatomyosistis, a rare autoimmune disease. One in three million people have it. Well, isn't that lucky for me? It can take two tracks. One is dermatological, resulting in skin disorders. The other, enzymes infiltrate the muscles in the body which can instantly take away the ability to lift your muscles. Ultimately, when it prevents swallowing, the patient dies.

Shortly after being diagnosed, I was in so much pain I couldn't walk to the next room. Steve and I were thinking it would be sucky to live with him waiting on me hand and foot for the rest of our lives. I hated asking for help with anything.

There I go, getting that humbleness and pride lesson again. Life has taught me to ask the appropriate question, "What am I supposed to learn from this experience?" That prompted me to take a complete inventory of my life. What do I want to do with the rest of it? What do I need to eliminate? What if I only have thirty days to live?

I immediately stopped doing things just because I thought I should. I stopped letting other people control my time with things they should be doing for themselves. I did an accounting of my life choices, and determined that I had made some good ones that I could be proud of. I realized that my time was my time.

I had walked an incredible journey through many soul wounds and came out with a stronger relationship with God. I became connected with the Universe in a beautiful way. I have always been loved!

I had choices about how to respond to my diagnosis. I decided to combine modern and alternative medicine. The specifics of the process would unfold. I entered into a new phase in my life; my accumulated knowledge would support me in my journey through the unknown areas of the diagnosis. I was in acceptance of what the moment brought. I was determined not to struggle against life, but go with the flow of life.

The creation of this book has been a hard journey for me. I had to die to myself to live again. Through the process of writing this book, I found a softness and compassion. With the death of my daughter, I realized that each day is precious and I am grateful for the journey that I took.

Like many sexually molested children, Tammy kept her secret until she was thirty five. Also, like most abused children, the consequence of her molestation put her on the path of drug addiction, and eventually prison. I recognize she also made many decisions that perpetuated her addiction. Our journey took us on the road to hell and back that no family wants to travel.

Shamanic Breathwork

I was looking forward to a new adventure, attending a shamanic breathwork class. Fourteen of us joined in a circle that opened the day with a ceremony and an invitation to connect with the Universe. I liked the ritual; it seemed like a great way to set our intention for the day. We picked partners to work with, and each of us had blankets to lie on. The music began with a disjointed heavy rhythm; it seemed earthy.

Quickly, I found myself dropping down into a trance; I could smell the earth and feel hoof beats on the ground. I realized the hooves were mine.

I was a gazelle, running with my feet barely touching the ground. I could feel the breeze on my face, as my hooves skimmed the earth. I could smell the sweet smell of grass and feel the sun on my skin. I was one with the wind, the sun and my body. I could feel my muscles as they stretched out, working in harmony. Words cannot describe the incredible joy of being connected with the earth.

Suddenly, there was a shift in the music, and I was with the tribal elders preparing me for a "rite of passage" ceremony. I was a little nervous, not sure what I was going to be doing. The tribe seemed to know what was coming; their attitude was grave. They were singing songs and beating drums; all of the tribe was immersed in activity. I was still a gazelle. Other members of the tribe were different animals. Animal power and energy entered the circle by the fire. We danced around the fire in the flickering firelight.

The next thing I knew, I was being sucked down into the earth. I had no idea what my body was; I just existed. I could feel the darkness, the dampness of the earth; I was going down, down, down, to total pitch black darkness.

Suddenly, I felt sick and cold. There was nothing but an engulfing blackness. I sensed this was an evil place. I was searching for something. As I searched, I knew I was being watched by a dark energy and it felt creepy. Unexpectedly, I came to a cavern which I instantly recognized as the "cave of darkness," This place where the "dark one" keeps the souls of children who have been sexually abused. I recognized this as the place where Raymond sometimes came to retrieve souls.

I was confused; I didn't know why I was here? I looked out over the cave and saw a multitude of children. Suddenly with a nauseating wave, I felt their anguish. I felt their pain in my body and soul. The intensity of the grief made me hot and sweaty. I was absorbing the emotions of all the children. I was physically ill; I wanted to throw up. I felt defiled and shamed. This was a shame so great I wanted to hide.

Instantly, I was holding my baby in my arms who I knew had been sexually abused and defiled. Who would do such a thing to a precious innocent baby? Tammy was in my arms and a deep grief emerged from my soul. I was trapped in my mind, body and soul, and then I released a primal scream that contained the depth of despair at losing my baby.

I began to tremble and cry sorrowfully. My tears flowed for all abused children and especially for my baby. How could I be separated from this baby of mine? I didn't even know this severe grief existed. I cried until I was limp.

As quickly as I went down into the darkness of the bowels of the earth, I came up. When I arrived at the surface, I was met by a fire which started at my feet, rolled up to the top of my body and to my head. The fire felt astonishingly good.

It was burning away the defilement of the abused children; burning away the shame, the anger, and the hurt. Tears fell as I welcomed it. I took in a deep cleansing breath, and then became nothing but a skeleton. Next, surrounded by a blue light, a bubble of God's love, I could feel a blessed healing enter me.

A peace came over my soul. I could experience God's love, and so could the children. As suddenly as I went into the earth, I entered into the night sky and could see the stars set in the dark sky. The moon was shining crystal clear.

Then I was back with my tribe. The wolves were circling me, protecting me, and the Indians were dancing the dance of celebration, the dance of life. I was tired and fell into a deep restful sleep. I was changed.

My Comments:

This was probably one of the most transformational experiences I have ever had. It made me recognize humans grieve on different levels, and sometimes have to drill down to get to the bottom of it. I had grieved the loss of Tammy as my child, but this time needed to grieve the loss of Tammy as my baby.

The encounter with the sexually abused children gave me an experiential appreciation of the defilement sexual abuse puts upon a child. I came out of this shamanic breathwork with enormous compassion for myself and for the beautiful children.

Mayo Clinic

I went to Mayo Clinic at Rochester, Minnesota where my diagnosis of Dermatomyosistis was confirmed. The hospital was huge with people bustling in every direction. They have an elaborate system in which they set you up with various evaluations and appointments in different departments. After evaluations are reviewed by the staff, they bring all the information to one place to discuss your particular situation.

What impressed me the most as I walked through the hallways were families and friends pushing wheelchairs and helping the ill. Their dedication was admirable, as they often had to wait hours for their loved ones' appointments. Their life had been turned upside down by someone else's illness, yet they supported their loved ones in every way possible. Volunteers came to sing in the atrium. Beautiful music echoed through the hallways as people gathered to watch. Other volunteers assisted people in getting from place to place. There was a helpful spirit at the clinic, dear to the heart.

Stress was also a part of the Mayo Clinic experience. Many people didn't know the specifics of their illness when they came to the clinic, and being away from home added further stress. Different tests were physically stressful; and sometimes you could see fear on the patient's faces. Many patients were older and in poor health, yet, resiliency and hope was in the air.

All of my appointments were finished, except one in the Pulmonary Department. When I wrapped it up, I could go back to Illinois. I was ready to be home. I needed this one final appointment. Four days in a row I went back to the clinic to see if they could work me in. "I hope today is my lucky day," I thought, as I checked in at the desk. They told me to take a seat and wait, and they would see if there was an opening. The waiting room was packed; I wasn't thinking an opening was going to happen for me again.

As I was sitting; a man who looked to be in his forties, took a seat right next to me. He looked thin, gaunt and stressed. He was talking on the phone to his wife. I felt uncomfortable because I couldn't help but overhear his conversation. She had stayed home because they couldn't afford for both of them to come. Apparently, he had been out of work for the last two years, and in and out of the doctor's office. No one could figure out what was wrong with him. I could hear the homesickness in his voice.

He asked his wife how things were going at church, so I assumed he must be a man of faith. I hoped it was getting him through this tough time in his life. Then I heard him tell his wife that he prayed that morning that he would get ill while he was at Mayo Clinic. Well, that was a shock for me. Who prays to get ill? He wanted the doctors to see what was going on with him. My heart went out to him; I knew he was desperate for help. I wondered about his life lessons.

I kept getting a persistent feeling I should pray for this man which I tried to ignore. When he was off the phone, I apologized, saying that I couldn't help but overhear his conversation. I asked if I could pray for him. He replied, "Would you really do that for me?"

I began to pray quietly in the waiting room. I prayed, *"God, give him courage, strength, and faith. God, please pick his doctors by hand, ones that could help him. God, please take care of this family, and lift the blanket of defeatism from his soul."*

As quickly as the prayer was finished, I heard my name being called, and the receptionist said the doctor could see me. I then heard his name called and the receptionist saying, "I'm sorry, we'll not be able to see you today." He went his way and I went mine. I had a profound impression that the morning was not an accident, but a meeting set up by the Universe.

Pterodactyl Era

I scheduled an appointment with Teri, my sound therapist and her mentor, Cheryl, who was here from out of state. I was looking forward to the appointment because I knew Cheryl did reflexology. Ever since I had been hit by the car, my feet were a mess. They constantly cramped and were painful. I wondered if my feet hurt so badly after the accident because the flow of energy in my body had been disrupted. I realized from seeing reflexology charts that points on the feet connect with every body organ.

After thinking about my intention for the meeting, I decided to address my diagnosis of Dermatomyosistis. The last several months my hands had been breaking out terribly, along with newly appearing eruptions around my eyes. Every eruption that flares up stays and never goes away.

I shared my intention with Cheryl and Teri. Teri began to get information about the C-3 and C-4 areas of my spine, while Cheryl pushed on the pressure points of my feet. My feet were locked and inflexible, particularly the big toe and the next. Cheryl continued manipulating the energy in my feet, while Teri manipulated the energy at my neck.

Teri then began to tune into my illness. It appeared to her as a simmering cauldron under the skin. It was boiling, and rolling. She intuitively saw trauma that I'd picked up from my loved ones, which was trapped and unable to escape from under my skin. In my mind I was laughing and thinking what a great metaphor for the eruptions and boils under my skin with the diagnosis of Dermatomyosistis.

Teri and Cheryl facilitated the movement of energy. My energy began to unlock and move, releasing the blocked energy. Teri picked up a didgeridoo and played deep earthy music. I felt the music in my body, and relaxed even further into the earth, a place that surrounded, supported and protected me. As I smelled the earth I became a part of it. It cradled and rocked me. I was so comfortable there.

The next thing I knew, I was surrounded by a golden bubble of light with a fire starting at the bottom of my feet that began to roll over my body. It was purifying my body. Ashes dropped at my feet, as I thanked the fire. What a curiosity. It shouldn't feel good but it did.

I enter into a still place of nothingness, floating and drifting. I am just a heart beating. Time suspended and did not exist. I was one with infinity, the beginning and the end. Do not disturb me; I do not want to leave this place.

Teri began drumming persistently and insistently. Cheryl came to another inflexible place in my feet, it was rigid and stiff. She described it as if I was stuck somewhere. I've heard that before. Lying at the table, the thought came to me that my body was thrown out of its own timing in after being hit by the car. I didn't know how to recover my timing.

I told Cheryl I had hammertoe surgery on two toes. She asked me if they were up or down and I replied they were up. She said that goes back to the Pterodactyl Era.

Suddenly, I found myself in that distant timeline and was stuck between a rock and a hard spot; I couldn't go up or down. I couldn't go backward or forward, I was simply stuck. Teri also saw me at the beginning of time, when a shift in the earth had occurred. I missed the shift; missed my timing.

Cheryl continued working on my feet until she felt a release, and I sensed a shift in my body. Teri then began to play the tuning forks, touching each foot, sending their vibrations to realign my vibrations. Too soon and from a distance, I heard a voice gently and quietly calling me back to the room. I was tired and needed to sleep.

My Comments:

It took several weeks for me to integrate this particular sound therapy. My first awareness of improvement came when I started writing a check and realized that some of my old hand writing had returned. Ever since the accident, I had difficulty with writing and transposing letters. Now my writing and spelling was much improved.

Next I went to take Houdini (my sister's dog) for a bicycle ride. I jumped on the bike with more balance and ease. I became conscious that there had been a great shift in my coordination and balance. All of a sudden I realized I am more like the old me. As I was assimilating all of this information, I came to a new awareness - that I had been knocked into another time reality when I was struck by the car. I had moved energetically back to the beginning of time.

Sound therapy had incredibly shifted my energy back into my own timing in this lifetime. I am the old new me. I am so grateful to God for bringing me to this place with understanding.

Family

Steve and I, Stephanie and the grandchildren went to the beach in Alabama and were looking over the ocean. Steve and I stood on the shore, as Stephanie and the children jumped into kayaks and peddled out into the water. I was amazed that Morgan was not afraid; she had taken an astonishing healing journey.

They began setting a nice pace. Amazingly, dolphins popped out of the water right next to the kids kayaks. They could reach out and touch the dolphins. Together, the children and dolphins paddled and swam, laughing and splashing in the water.

I smiled; somehow I knew my daughter Tammy had orchestrated this day from the other side. My golden heart swelled with love, knowing Tammy was no longer in pain. I smiled as I knew Stephanie and my grandchildren would be alright and that the pieces of our lives had been put back together.

That same day Raymond called to tell me he was ready to speak at the school about drugs. I wished him luck, knowing that he would find the right words to touch the children's hearts. I sat down by the ocean to fill out my gratitude journal.

Gratitude Journal

I am grateful for:

- ♥ My husband Steve - he is the rock who weathered the storms, and still stands majestically tall.

- ♥ Tammy - she taught me to forgive, and that we have free will in responding to life. She was brave to choose her life's experiences for her soul's growth.

- ♥ Stephanie - she taught me independence and courage.

- ♥ My grandson Stephen Ray - he taught me the value of tenacity and survival.

- ♥ My grandson Zachary - he taught me the value of being in the moment.

- ♥ Granddaughters Amber, Morgan, and Cheyenne - they taught me the importance of the trust of a child.

- ♥ My Father and Mother - they taught me about unconditional love, and were wonderful role models.

- ♥ My sisters and brother - they love and support me and are always truthful with me.

- ♥ Raymond - he taught me courage in the face of adversity. He connected me with my ancestors.

- ♥ For night – it produces some of my most creative moments.

- ♥ My health - it taught me I had to lose it to appreciate it.
- ♥ Experiencing grief – I learned it is okay to be vulnerable.
- ♥ Experiencing physical pain and trauma - it gave me the opportunity to look deeper and heal the painful parts of my life.
- ♥ Experiencing sorrow and sadness – I learned the value of laughter and happiness.
- ♥ All the healers who have been drawn into my life - they have taught me value of universal connection.
- ♥ A broken heart – I learned about the value of love for healing.
- ♥ For getting hit by a car - it taught me the mind/body connection in the role of healing.
- ♥ For loosing thirteen of my relatives in one year - it taught me the preciousness of life, and that we are still connected to the other side.
- ♥ To my spirit guides, angels, and ascended masters - they inform my life daily and never give up on me.
- ♥ God - He taught me lessons, pushed me to grow, has always been in control, loves me and gave me a golden heart.

Stillness

~Sharron Magyar

In the stillness, the breeze brushes across my face
Wind silently plays with my hair.
Sun travels down my body, warming me in this space,
My heart silently healing in time with this place.
I can feel the air going in my chest, bringing life to me,
Breath and heart listening to the still.
Dropping down into the silence,
When I know all things I fight for.
And all pain is in vain,
Listening to my breath, just knowing I am.

Final Note

I can only encourage you if you have been sexually abused to find someone safe to tell. It is in telling your story that the energy which has been held in your body and subconscious can be released. If you can't find anyone to tell, you are welcome to write me about it. I cannot promise to answer every letter, but I do promise your letter will be read and given honor.